ON THE ROAD TO
VEGETARIAN COOKING

Merry Christmas Marc —

for that on-going streak of successful dinner parties!

xo
love Kel

ON THE ROAD TO
VEGETARIAN COOKING

Easy Meals for Everyone

by

Anne Lukin

SECOND STORY Press

CANADIAN CATALOGUING IN PUBLICATION DATA
Lukin, Anne
On the road to vegetarian cooking

Includes index
ISBN 0-929005-28-7

1. Cookery (Vegetables).   2. Vegetarianism.
1. Title.

TX837.L85 1991   641.5'636   C91-094895-X

Illustrations by Laurie Lafrance
Printed and bound in Canada

Published by
SECOND STORY PRESS
760 Bathurst St
Toronto, Ontario
M5S 2R6

CONTENTS

INTRODUCTION

SOUPS, SALADS AND SIDE DISHES

SOUPS

SALADS

GRAINS

QUICK MEALS

BAKING, BREAKFASTS AND BRUNCH TREATS

ACKNOWLEDGEMENTS

To my family, who shaped my earliest memories of food...from those early mashed-potato competitions with my brothers, to holiday meals with the extended family where feasts unravelled into long-winded, and long-cherished, stories.

And to my parents, Edward Keith and Allie Leeth Lukin, who kept food on the table and didn't wring our necks when we wouldn't eat it.

To my friends, who make it worthwhile.

To Second Story Press, whose continued support, hard work, professionalism, and experience made this book possible.

To Barbara Mains, the editor, whose steady and expert hand at the editorial helm rescued this book from the doldrums of deadlines and kept it off the rocky shores of run-on sentences.

To Laurie Lafrance, whose vibrant and wonderful illustrations come to life on the page, and make the book look good enough to eat.

To the test-cooks, and taste-testers: Mary Helen Kolisnyk, Dann McCann, Lorraine Newman, Jen Norfolk, Ann Rowan, David Smith, Ilse Turnsen, Mordecai Wasserman and the Markhams.

To Miriam Hoffer and Dahna Birkson, for lending their expertise in diet and nutrition, and to the other friends who read the manuscript and gave helpful feedback.

To Maureen McLaughlin, for proofing and correcting ad infinitum.

And to Dann McCann, Sheri Bishop, John Ghitan, and the Markhams for their day-to-day support and friendship, even through the blackest periods of my whining about how much I hate to stick to recipes and deadlines.

Thanks!

And to the reader; I hope you will find this book encouraging and helpful in planning, cooking and eating more vegetarian meals.

Most of all I hope you find a few recipes that you really love to eat, and that you get to share the food with people you love.

Anne Lukin
August 1991

INTRODUCTION

CULINARY CONFESSIONS OF A CLOSET CARNIVORE

I've cooked professionally over the last 12 years as a vegetarian cook. I've eaten and enjoyed a lot of delicious meatless meals. I've also created hundreds of vegetarian recipes. When I cook for myself, it's nearly always a vegetarian meal. But here's the confession, I still – sometimes – eat meat.

I wrote this cookbook for each and every one of us on the road to vegetarian cooking. You may already be a seasoned traveller in the land of tofu and grains, or you may be standing at the signpost, wondering if this is a route you'd like to explore. I want to share with you some of my reasons for eating vegetarian meals, and some of the vegetarian recipes that I've created over the years.

I'm confessing right from the start that I still – sometimes! – eat meat, in the hope that those of you who are not yet vegetarians will see that you can begin to change your diet without having to do it radically overnight. You can eat meatless meals – occasionally or often – without having to give up entirely on your favourite meat entrées. This cookbook has been designed to ease your transition from old favourites to new, vegetarian discoveries.

So why do I still eat meat? Because certain social occasions may be awkward for non-meat-eaters, and I don't always choose to rock the boat. Because I still crave bacon, a childhood favourite (I know, I know, bacon is *not* health food). And because – here comes the truth – I may not be the world's most disciplined person when it comes to diet.

But I do recognize very clearly that vegetarian food is healthier – it's lighter, better for me, and doesn't clog my veins with cholesterol the way meat does. I'm uncomfortable when I stop to think about what happens to cows, chickens, and pigs before they're parcelled into those tightly wrapped packages at the meat counter. And sometimes I'm moved to think of the large percentage of the world's population that goes to bed hungry every night. Such images provide the stick that have driven this proverbial donkey on the road to a vegetarian diet.

And the carrot that leads me on? I love to eat. I come from a long line of eaters. The branch of my family with Eastern European Jewish roots expressed its love with matzo ball soup and latkes and brisket and mandelbrot. Other relatives, Southerners and farmers, lavished me with fried chicken, mashed potatoes, and chocolate meringue pie. What the two traditions held in common was the unstated conviction that if you loved someone, you fed them. To return love was to eat and appreciate. Food was sustenance and nurturing, solace and celebration.

My culinary heritage has been further enriched by all the places I've lived, beginning with the the enchiladas and fiery salsa of my Tex-Mex childhood, all the way to the succulent dumplings, soups and stirfried glories of Toronto's Chinatown.

So, I like to cook. I like to talk about food and to invent new dishes. And you know what? Vegetarian food lends itself to that passion every bit as well as meat. There are so many intriguing new possibilities in the world of vegetarian cooking. It's turned out to be a wonderful adventure for this cook to expand her knowledge and repertoire of meatless meals — and an unending source of delight to this diner.

No one can say that there is only one right way to eat. But more and more people are beginning to look critically at the impact of the typical North American diet upon our health. Researchers increasingly link this diet to a high national incidence of heart disease, cancer, and stroke. The connection between our health and our place in the food chain is cause for deep concern, given the quantity and number of chemicals in the air and water, as well as in livestock feed. A growing body of material documents the reasons why many people are beginning to turn away from meat as a major component of their diet. (See the bibliography for several examples.)

Perhaps you are already a vegetarian, looking for fresh ideas and some advice about unfamiliar ingredients. Perhaps you currently eat meat, but for health, ethical, or economic reasons, you'd like to start preparing meatless meals. Or you may not be interested in changing your own diet, but you have a friend or family member who is a vegetarian, and you want to know what on earth to feed them when they come for dinner. Read on!

There are a lot of misconceptions about vegetarian food, that it has to be brown and heavy and boring and virtuous. And I've certainly been served some of the disasters that gave vegetarian food its erstwhile, if undeserved, reputation for weirdness. I cringe to recall, for instance, a convention banquet at which the vegetarian option was "Oatloaf". (Perhaps we'll pause here in a moment of silent meditation for that all-too-memorable creation. Yes, it was every bit as dreary as it sounds...Sort of like baked oatmeal laced with ketchup. I did **not** ask for the recipe...) And yet, I'm sure the caterers were sincerely trying to produce a meatless dish to satisfy vegetarians. They just didn't succeed. Maybe they needed a cookbook like this one.

Maybe they needed *this* cookbook.

The recipes that follow provide a starter kit of comfortable, familiar foods for everyday meals, as well as several exotic dishes for those nights when you've got the time to visit new culinary territory. Ingredients to tantalize your tastebuds! Suggestions for superfast vegetarian lunches and dinners, for making your own vegetarian convenience foods, and for stocking your kitchen. Congratulations! You're well on the road to vegetarian cooking.

WHY EAT VEGETARIAN?

Ask vegetarians why they don't eat meat, and many would tell you that that they're concerned about its effect on their health. Some will specify cholesterol and saturated fats. There, we've brought out the buzzwords. You're probably aware of the dangers of cholesterol and saturated fats in your diet, and the associated risk of heart disease, stroke, or other illnesses. But buzzwords get thrown at us so often and so fast these days, let's take a minute to unravel them.

Negative press aside, cholesterol is not all bad. In fact, it is one of your body's essential building blocks. Your liver produces one type, called **blood cholesterol**, which your arteries deliver around your body to build cells and to manufacture vitamin D and various hormones. You add another type to your body when you eat certain foods. **Dietary cholesterol**, present in animal-based foods such as meat, dairy products, poultry, and fish, can adversely affect your levels of blood cholesterol. While you do need some cholesterol in your blood, too much may contribute to heart disease in some people. The arteries that supply the blood to keep your heart working may become clogged with fatty deposits from too much cholesterol and saturated fat. This condition is called atherosclerosis; when the arteries close off completely, a heart attack may result. The same condition can cause a stroke, when the arteries affected are those that lead to the brain.

Other factors can affect your cholesterol levels and general health: the amount of saturated fats and total fat in your diet, your gender, age, and weight, the amount of exercise or physical activity in your life, smoking, alcohol, stress, and your family medical history.

Our bodies develop very individualized responses to cholesterol. For some people cholesterol-laden food is not a danger, because their bodies process it well. Other people inherit bodies which cannot process dietary cholesterol efficiently. Regardless of your heredity, it is probably still a good idea to cut down on dietary cholesterol. And it is equally important to reduce total fat intake, especially saturated fats. Meat is a major contributor of total fats, saturated fat, and cholesterol, so the easiest way to decrease the consumption of these is to decrease the consumption of meat. By its very nature, a vegetarian diet can be very low in fat, especially if you restrict or eliminate fried foods and high-fat dairy products, and if you're sparing in your use of butter and oils for cooking.

The **only** way to add cholesterol to your body is to eat meat, poultry or fish, dairy products, or eggs. Food from plant sources is entirely free of dietary cholesterol. And most foods from plant sources are low in saturated fats, while meat products tend to be high in saturated fats. (The exceptions are palm or palm kernel or coconut oils, and chocolates – these contain saturated fats.) Polyunsaturated oils such as corn, safflower, sunflower, and soybean oils, and mono-unsaturated oils like olive or peanut oils, can actually help reduce blood cholesterol.

The good news is that changing your diet to reduce your total fat intake and reduce your consumption of saturated fats and dietary cholesterol can help lower your blood cholesterol levels, thereby reducing the risk of atherosclerosis and other health risks. But this probably isn't news to you. If your own doctor hasn't mentioned it, you've certainly read it on the back of a breakfast cereal box or heard it in a margarine commercial.

Nor is atherosclerosis the only reason to modify your diet. We know that diet influences health, for good or ill. The health benefits from vegetarianism include decreased risk of obesity, non-insulin dependent diabetes, hypertension, gallstones, and diverticular disease. A vegetarian diet can also reduce the risk of certain forms of cancer.

So getting beyond the buzzwords, what does this mean for your breakfast bowl, your lunch box, and your dinner plate? It means cutting down on high-fat dairy products, cutting out meat and poultry, and eating more fresh vegetables and grains. Sounds like a vegetarian menu to me! Especially when you consider that vegetarian staples such as dried beans, dried peas, and oat bran contain soluble fibre, which actually helps your body to **reduce** its cholesterol levels. Fresh vegetables and the bran of whole wheat further enrich a vegetarian diet with insoluble fibre, which is vital to digestion.

And there's a bonus: a vegetarian meal, since it is largely made from scratch with fresh ingredients, tends to contain few preservatives or chemical additives. (Perhaps you already have the habit of reading labels on cans and boxes: half the ingredients are unpronounceable, and the only thing longer than the list of unpronounceable ingredients may be the shelf-life of the "food" itself.)

FOOD AS FUEL

Most of us these days lead hectic, stress-filled lives, with multiple demands on our minds and bodies. We juggle work, school, family schedules, deadlines, relationships, housework, finances, exercise (and guilt at not exercising enough!). Sound familiar? Modern life asks us to toss a lot of balls up into the air – and keep them moving.

Now, stop and think about what you put into your body as fuel for the mad race you run every day. Many of us expect our bodies to function on coffee and donuts, soft drinks, chips, and a frozen dinner microwaved at the end of the day. And then we wonder why we feel tired and stressed! If you put sugar in a car's gas tank the way most people put sugar into their bodies every day in a refined-foods diet, that car wouldn't leave the driveway. Why not give your body the advantage of useful, usable food for fuel to carry you through not only each hectic day, but a long lifetime of days.

Have I mentioned yet that I love to eat? I've actually been accused of living to eat. Food is a major source of pleasure in my life, and the impetus for my favourite social rituals. But I have friends for whom food holds little interest, who view it largely as a necessary nuisance. Whether you "eat to live", or "live to eat", you still depend on food for fuel, nourishment, life force. It's one of the basics that we all work to provide ourselves and our families with. Doesn't it make sense to choose your energy sources from food that is fresh, healthy, and nutritious, instead of from food that is processed, sprayed, sugared, dyed, preserved, and irradiated?

There are sound economic reasons for eating vegetarian meals. Vegetarian dinners made from low-cost staples such as beans and grains are bound to be cheaper than meat alternatives, especially with the high cost of red meat. Even if you're not prepared to commit to an exclusively vegetarian diet today, you may want to experiment with one or more meatless meals a week, simply to stretch your grocery dollar.

Personal concerns about your health or household budget are not the only reasons for choosing the vegetarian option. There's a world of pressing issues: equitable distribution, global resources, the imperative of sustainable agriculture, the treatment of sentient creatures on their way to becoming food. If you are interested in these issues, I urge you to read: *Diet for a Small Planet* by Frances Moore Lappé, and John Robbins' *Diet for a New America*.

Lappé calculates that it takes about 16 pounds of grain to produce each pound of beef; it also takes a considerable amount of water, to raise the cow as well as the grain to feed the cow. The terrible problem of world hunger meanwhile worsens. We continue to squander valuable resources that could feed the many, so that the few can be sure of their daily allotment of meat (with its corresponding heart and weight problems). This grim picture has been made bleaker yet by the ongoing destruction of the South American rain forests: this incredibly precious ingredient in the ecological balance is being destroyed to accomodate massive cattle ranges. The simple truth is that if more people around the world ate grains and vegetables instead of meat, *more people around the world would eat.*

ANIMAL RIGHTS AND WELFARE

Many of us share growing ethical concerns about the treatment of farm animals before they end up on our plates. It's all too easy to think of beef, poultry, or pork as commodities, ingredients without a past. We are encouraged to think of it in these terms because it comes so neatly wrapped in transparent plastic, bearing no signs of struggle. In *Diet for a New America*, John Robbins outlines the harsh realities that precede the saran-wrapped packages. Well-cared-for calves munching grass while perky hens scratch nearby are largely a thing of children's book illustrations. The unpleasant truth is that in contemporary agribusiness, animals are treated like so much raw material, to be processed with the least expense and difficulty for the greatest financial return. The realities of large-scale livestock production are severe overcrowding and mutilation: a life lived in fear in a highly artificial environment, removed from natural surroundings and diets. Remember that the hormones and antibiotics pumped into livestock will make their way into human tissue when we eat these treated – and mistreated – animals.

Compelling reasons to stop eating meat, or at least to cut down on it as much as possible. For those occasions when you still serve meat, find a reputable supplier of organic, free-range meat; it will be free of additives, and the animals will have led more normal lives. Check your natural foods store or farmers' market for free-range eggs and organic produce: you'll be supporting local growers at the same time.

Reasons aplenty to give serious thought about what's on your plate and how it got there. Far too many North Americans eat without thinking, putting into their mouths what's convenient, or trendy. It's hard to resist the slick and persuasive food imagery with which we're bombarded by TV, magazine, and supermarket advertising. The sophisticated campaigns of multinational corporations and marketing boards effectively tap our food nostalgia, as well as our anxieties about health. Supermarket shelves are crowded with "natural" products, including mass-produced "granola bars" with chocolate chips, corn syrup, and the shelf life of a year. "Cholesterol-free" frozen french fries are another example; the irony is that while they are free of cholesterol, they are not free of fat. They offer more in the way of convenience than they do nutritional value.

We are not doing our bodies any favour when we eat without thinking, without examining the content of the food we eat, or the context of the choices we make about food. If food is the very stuff of life, do we really want to live a "fast food existence"?

I've touched briefly on the many reasons for turning away from a steady diet of meat. But I shouldn't neglect to mention some of the delightful, exciting, delicious reasons for choosing a vegetarian diet. For those of us who grew up on the traditional, western diet of meat-and-potatoes, vegetarian cuisine represents a whole world of discoveries. Many cultures have specialized in vegetarian cooking for centuries, developing subtle and tantalizing combinations of ingredients. Vegetarian cooking is an invitation to adventure.

No matter how far down the road to a vegetarian lifestyle you find yourself, it's wise to remember that food is a very personal issue. People can be very idiosyncratic and emphatic about food, rooted as it is in both emotional and political connotations. "Food fascists" who insist that others share their food choices are unlikely to win converts. Respect for the other person, sharing, and enjoying works a lot better.

In that spirit, *bon appetit!*

WHAT DO VEGETARIANS EAT?

Some people simply can't imagine a dinner plate without a meat-based entrée front and centre. "What do vegetarians eat?!?," I've been asked. "Almost everything that wouldn't eat them first," is one response. The list of options for vegetarians is extensive and varied enough to delight any gourmet.

Many cultural groups around the world have lived as vegetarians for centuries, so that we have rich culinary traditions to enjoy. Some have not had the luxury of an economy or a climate that lent itself to the production of meat. Others refrain from eating meat for religious or moral reasons.

In Japan tofu is a daily dish, eaten with vegetables like daikon radish, squash or bean sprouts, and noodles called udon or soba. In Italy one would sit down to a plate of pasta primavera during Lent with fresh peas and young greens. In India, lentils, split peas, and rice are served alongside spinach, potatoes, and homemade cheese. Millet, peanuts, tomatoes, and okra are staples in northern Africa. Most cuisines have traditional combinations which unconsciously provide protein complements: tortillas and beans, rice and tofu, nuts and grains.

In North America, a healthy vegetarian diet is made up of a balanced mix of fresh vegetables and fruit, grains, nuts, beans, soy products like tofu and tempeh, and sometimes cheese, milk, and eggs. We've borrowed from other cultures, and created traditions of our own. There may be a main entrée, such as lasagna, or tempeh burgers, or the meal may consist of a couple of salads or vegetable dishes that go well together. Like meat eaters, vegetarians eat casseroles, soups, sandwichs, salads, and favourites like spaghetti, pizza, and tacos. And even desserts!

Different kinds of vegetarians follow different diets. In fact, some days I think there are as many degrees of vegetarianism as there are people who don't eat meat. This reflects the fact that food is a very personal matter, with a different meaning for each person.

For the purpose of this book, we will define a vegetarian as **someone who does not eat meat**: beef or veal, chicken, pork, lamb or mutton, game, fish, shellfish, etc. (Many people have chosen not to eat red meat but still occasionally consume chicken or fish. Strictly speaking, their diet would not qualify as vegetarian. Chicken and fish, while they do not have the soulful eyes of a calf, are still sentient creatures, and therefore not part of a vegetarian diet.)

Vegetarians themselves are split into two main groups: those who eat eggs and dairy products, and those who don't. The ones who do are sometimes referred to as ovo-lacto vegetarians (ovo = eggs, lacto = milk). People who follow a stricter vegetarian diet are called vegans. A vegan diet excludes the use of any product derived from sentient creatures: flesh, milk, eggs, or honey. Some vegans feel strongly enough about the rights of animals that they choose not to use any part of an animal for any purpose, including leather (the hide of an animal) or glue (commonly made by boiling hooves and bones). Other people may have given up eggs or milk because of cholesterol, or the inability to digest dairy products. (Many books are available at your library or natural foods store with further information on both vegan principles and dairy allergies).

Another term you may have heard in connection with the vegetarian lifestyle is *macrobiotics*. Developed in Japan by Georges Ohsawa, macrobiotics is both a philosophy of living and a set of dietary principles. A macrobiotic diet consists of local, seasonal food, simply prepared. Macrobiotic principles encourage individuals to develop their own diet toward the end goal of achieving maximum health and harmony with the environment. (Consult the bibliography for selected titles on macrobiotic philosophy and cooking.)

There are a number of ways to begin to live as a vegetarian, and one is right for you. You might begin by cutting down your consumption of red meat, or by choosing chicken and fish instead. Some people experience an overnight revolution in their thinking about food and plunge headfirst into the vegetarian way of life. Others are ordered by their doctors to eliminate cholesterol and fat. Whatever put you on the road to vegetarian cooking, and wherever you find yourself on the path, remember that a vegetarian diet is not a fad. It is a set of conscious choices about what you consume. You are free to change what you eat, and to re-examine those choices and make new ones, at any time. Hopefully, vegetarian meals will be a lifelong choice for you, with a lifetime of dividends.

Going without meat is decidedly NOT a diet of deprivation or sacrifice. It is a world of exciting flavours, tantalizing aromas, vibrant colours, and succulent textures. These may not be the flavours or foods of your childhood. But if the tastes you grew up with are clogging your arteries, weighing you down, or just boring you occasionally, then keep reading.

MEALS WITHOUT MEAT – THE PROTEIN ISSUE

People eat meat from habit, custom, tradition, and as a way of proving to themselves and to others that they can afford it. And they also eat meat for the way it tastes, and for protein. Habits can always be changed, new traditions forged. While nothing exactly replaces the taste of meat, there are plenty of delicious, and habit-forming, alternatives. Many long-time vegetarians, in fact, find that the flavour of meat loses its appeal over time.

But what about protein?

A lot of people worry – needlessly – about getting sufficient protein without meat. Two factors contribute to this alarm. The first is conditioning, pure and simple. We lived a lot of years when our nutritional "needs" were defined by beef marketing boards, and our culinary "wants" were shaped by the notion that prosperity should be demonstrated by the number of times a week we ate meat.

The second factor emerged in the early seventies, when North Americans first began to experiment with vegetarianism on a widespread basis. The predominant theory taught that you *could* obtain sufficient protein from a vegetarian diet, but you had to pay very close attention to your diet to achieve this objective. The theory of protein complementarity (consumption of non-meat foods in specific combinations to obtain enough protein by combining amino acids) was endlessly discussed and fretted over. Today's research indicates that North Americans tend to eat far too *much* protein. Current findings on the synthesis of protein within the human body have demonstrated that most people getting enough calories by eating a balanced vegetarian diet will absorb as much protein as they need. Growing children and pregnant women have special needs and should eat foods that provide them with enough protein, vitamins, and minerals to meet their increased needs.

And now, the details: proteins are made up of specific combinations of amino acids. Proteins that contain the ratio of amino acids most easily used by the human body are described as perfect or complete; meat, eggs, and dairy products each supply this kind of protein in a tidy package. (Unfortunately that package comes wrapped with cholesterol and saturated fats.) There are other ways to achieve correct combinations of amino acids, so that your body can build the protein it needs. Beans, grains, nuts, and — to a lesser extent, even vegetables and fruits — all contain some of the necessary amino acids. When these foods are eaten, together in complementary combinations at the same meal or even over the period of one or two days, our bodies store amino acids to build the protein we need.

Frances Moore Lappé broke new ground on this subject with *Diet for a Small Planet* (1971). Referencing medical and nutritional studies, she proved that humans could indeed absorb sufficient protein, without eating meat, to thrive. Lappé designed a comprehensive plan for combining beans, grains, and nuts to obtain the proper combination of amino acids. Her work encouraged people to see vegetarianism as a viable option, but also left us with the notion that you would need to be a dietician or a chemist to calculate the correct combinations of food categories.

In the two decades since, public attitudes have caught up to research. Fewer and fewer people are wedded to the notion that meat, especially red beef, is absolutely necessary, or even healthy. Current research on nutrition indicates that we need not be obsessively careful of our diet to meet our protein needs. Lappé revised *Diet for a Small Planet* in 1981, updating readers on her continuing work with food and nutrition. We now know that the human body copes quite well on its own in building proteins, if given a sufficiently varied diet to work from. Your body can store amino acids and combine them over time to meet its protein needs, so there is no need to consume precise food combinations in the same meal. As Lappé wrote in the revised tenth anniversary edition of her book, "With a healthy varied diet, concern about protein complementarity is not necessary for most of us."

GETTING STARTED

One of the most-heard complaints of non-vegetarians who want to try meatless meals is that you don't know where to start. All the ingredients are unfamiliar, and even if you take the plunge and buy tofu, for example, it sits in your fridge and goes bad because you just don't know what to *do* with it. And then you throw it out and open a can of tuna or go out for a hamburger instead. Well, we can put an end to those "pre-vegetarian tofu jitters".

This chapter will help you learn about a few of vegetarian staples and how to make them a part of your daily menus.

Each section takes a typical vegetarian entree ingredient and tells you what it is, and how to work with it. Tips on storage and how it is sold are included. I'll start with basic information about the ingredient, and teach you one or two ways to use it very simply. Plus some hints on how to incorporate it into other dishes. Then we'll finish with a complete recipe featuring our chosen staple as a key ingredient.

The staples we'll cover are inexpensive, relatively easy to work with, and good sources of protein (either alone or when eaten in combination with other items). By the end of this chapter you'll be familiar with:

- **Tofu** – a low-fat protein source that is bland and white, like a cheese made from soymilk. Use in stirfrys, casseroles, sandwiches, etc.
- **Nuts and nut butters** – Nuts are an elegant way of adding protein to salads, casseroles, vegetable dishes or desserts. Use them whole, sliced, chopped, or ground into nut butter.
- **Beans** – Beans are versatile, filling and inexpensive; good sources of protein and soluble fibre which reduces blood cholesterol. Use beans in soups, salads, casseroles, as a side dish, and on and on. We'll look in particular at aduki beans; a small red bean that cooks in less than one hour, and is easily digestible.
- **Tempeh** – another soy product that makes a good meat substitute because of its high protein content and chewy texture. Use it in stirfrys, casseroles and salads.

Which is not to say that you will only be eating these foods as vegetarian. But these will give you a foundation on which to base your cooking at first. Once you are comfortable with what they are and how to work with them, your own creativity can take over.

TOFU

Tofu has somehow become a symbol of vegetarianism for many people. For some it is the high-protein, inexpensive stepping stone to a different diet. For other people, cubes of tofu make up a brick wall that they run into when they think of vegetarian meals. "Am I going to have to eat tofu?", they wail. "No way, not me."

One answer is that you could live a long life as a vegetarian and never *have* to eat tofu. Soyfoods like tofu and tempeh are an acquired taste. Their taste and texture are pretty different from anything we grew up with here in the western world. But they have been eaten for centuries in other countries, and they are an excellent source of protein with no fat or cholesterol. I have to admit I was pretty sceptical the first time I looked a block of tofu in the eye as a potential dinner. But I tried it several times prepared in different ways, and have learned to appreciate tofu and tempeh as versatile and inexpensive additions to my diet.

Tofu is made by a process very similar to cheese making, using the "milk" from cooked and ground soybeans that is then formed into cubes. The end product is a smooth, bland, slightly spongy block that is high in protein and low in fat. It can be used raw or sauteed or baked to add to stirfrys, casseroles, salads, sandwiches, desserts and more. Tofu is usually found packaged in plastic or sold loose in bulk in half-pound blocks in the produce cooler section of your local store – it has become so much more widely known here in the West in the last few years that it can now be found in most regular grocery stores.

USES

Tofu can be eaten raw, as is, but its bland taste and texture is sometimes not appealing at first to a North American palate. Until you learn to like tofu for its own merits, you may prefer to cook it or mix it with other ingredients. It comes in different textures, from very firm to an almost custard-like product called silken tofu. For all the recipes in this book you will want to find a brand that is pressed into a dense, firm block.

I tend to use tofu in one of two ways, as these are the ones I enjoy best. The method I use most frequently is marinating and baking tofu. See the first recipe below. The other way I most commonly eat tofu is to mash it and mix it with yogurt or mayonnaise and seasonings, much as you would make egg salad using your regular recipe, or the Curried Egg Salad on p. 160. The simplest sandwich spread is just to mash drained tofu with a few tablespoons tamari, nutritional yeast, diced green onion and a blended herb salt substitute. Again, an acquired taste, but one I've grown to really like.

PREPARATION

Tofu soaks up moisture, which makes it the perfect medium for sauces and marinades. But since it is stored in water, tofu must be pressed and drained before use. This process gives it a firmer texture and allows better absorption of the sauce or marinade. To press, centre the tofu on a plate or baking tray with a rim. Lay a plate on top of the tofu, and then place a weight, such as a heavy tin can, on top of the plate. Be sure the weight is evenly distributed, and heavy enough to press but not flatten the tofu. Set aside for 15 to 30 minutes, then remove the weight, drain the expressed water, and prepare the tofu as instructed.

STORAGE

Store tofu in the refrigerator for 3 days to a week. It should be kept under water, and the water should be drained and replaced every other day to keep the tofu fresh.

Tofu can also be frozen – it will keep for 6 weeks in the freezer. Freezing changes the texture of tofu to a more spongy consistency, ideal for recipes that call for a chewy texture. Thaw the frozen tofu by soaking in boiling water, then press, drain and use as desired.

The following are some examples of basic tofu recipes.

BAKED MARINATED TOFU

Add these tasty tofu cubes to stirfries, salads,
noodle or vegetable casseroles for extra protein.
Serve marinated slices of tofu as an entree over rice,
covered with a sauce (sweet and sour, gravy, tomato,
etc.). Baked tofu is firm and holds together well.

SERVES 4

2 (8 oz.) blocks tofu, pressed and
    drained, cut into ½" cubes or
    ¼" slices
3 T. tamari
1 T. oil
1 clove garlic, minced
1 t. minced fresh ginger

PREHEAT OVEN TO 400° F.
While the tofu drains, combine
the other ingredients in a bowl.
Marinate the tofu in the tamari
marinade (or the marinade of
your choice) for 15 minutes.
Place the marinated tofu on an
oiled baking sheet and bake for
15 to 20 minutes until the tofu
is well-browned and crispy
around the edges.

For the following recipe, use tofu that has been previously frozen; the chewier texture that results from freezing will go well with the tangy barbeque sauce. Thaw the tofu by leaving at room temperature for a few hours, or by soaking in hot water and pressing well to express the liquid.

BBQ TOFU

Serve hot between toasted buns, or with baked beans.
Good cold the next day in sandwiches. This technique
also works well with tempeh.

SERVES 4

2 blocks tofu, pressed and drained,
   cut into ½" slices
1½ to 2 cups BBQ sauce (bottled, or
   try the recipe on p. 200)

PREHEAT OVEN TO 375° F. Spread the bottom of a casserole pan with a layer of BBQ sauce. Lay out the tofu slices in the pan, and drench with the remaining sauce. Cover and bake for 20 minutes; uncover and bake for a further 10 to 15 minutes, until the tofu is slightly browned and bubbling in the sauce.

TOFU RANCHERA

If you're trying to avoid cholesterol, tofu may be substituted for eggs in this Southwestern classic. Serve with refried beans or home fries and extra tortillas on the side.

SERVES 4

1 T. oil
1 medium onion, finely diced
3 cloves garlic, minced
1 large tomato, finely diced
1 T. tomato paste
1 T. water
1½ T. chili powder
2 t. cumin
salt, pepper to taste
dash of Worchestershire and Tabasco

Heat oil in a skillet. Sauté onion, tomato and garlic with seasonings until onions are browned.

2 blocks tofu, pressed, drained and mashed
8 flour tortillas, warmed
    picante sauce (mild, medium or hot, to taste)
diced green onions (for garnish)

Add mashed tofu and sauté, stirring as if you were scrambling eggs, for 7 to 10 minutes. Meanwhile warm the tortillas in the oven or on a griddle. Spoon the sautéed tofu and vegetables into the warm tortillas, and add picante sauce as desired. The tortillas may be rolled up like a taco and held in the hand, or served flat like a crepe, to be eaten with a knife and fork.

NUTS AND NUT BUTTERS

Peanuts, walnuts, pecans, brazil nuts, hazelnuts, and cashews are popular in kitchens around the world in cooking and baking. A national staple in some countries (such as peanuts in many parts of Africa), nuts in some cultures are treats or luxuries. They appear in the shell as a traditional holiday decoration, or in such whimsical creations as elaborately shaped marzipan candy made from almond paste. Though nuts are high in calories, they can be a good source of both flavour and protein. (Seeds such as sunflower seeds and pine nuts are also nutritional sources of protein; sesame seeds are packed with calcium as well.)

Nut butters are spreadable pastes made from ground nuts. We're most familiar with peanut butter, although almond, cashew, sesame and hazelnut butters are now widely available. Natural foods stores sell nut butters in bulk, so you can experiment with small quantities. Nut butters may be expensive; remember that a little goes a long way. Delectable as a sandwich spread, nut butters also provide a flavourful base for sauces.

STORAGE

Nuts and seeds contain a great deal of oil, which is why they may turn rancid as they age. Nuts are best kept in airtight plastic containers in the freezer. (If you buy small quantities of nuts and use them quickly, airtight containers kept in the cupboard will do.) In nut butters, occasionally the oil will separate from the ground nuts: there's nothing wrong with the nut butter, but some strenuous stirring will be called for to put the oil and solids back together again.

COOKING

Nuts may be eaten raw, but their flavour is greatly enhanced by toasting. To toast, preheat oven to 400 degrees F. Spread out the nuts on a baking sheet with a rim. Bake for 5 to 10 minutes, stirring occasionally as the nuts near the edges will brown first. Watch carefully, because nuts burn easily, and they are too expensive and wonderful to waste. When the nuts are golden brown, remove from the oven. Allow to cool before chopping with a knife. If you use a food processor to chop nuts, process in brief controlled bursts or you may end up with homemade nut butter.

Toss nuts in salads for a protein boost. Sprinkle over casseroles, desserts, or vegetables to make any simple dish immediately elegant. (See recipes for Brazilian Peanut Stew, p. 138, Waldorf Salad, p. 80 or Pumpkin Gingerbread, p. 171 for more ways to use nuts and nut butters.)

For an exorbitantly luxurious treat, substitute pistachio butter and chopped pistachios for the peanut butter in your favourite peanut butter cookie recipe. Major joy.

PISTACHIO HONEY-GLAZED CARROTS

SERVES 4

4 cups sliced carrots

Steam carrots in a steamer over boiling water, covered, for 15 minutes or until just tender.

1 ½ T. oil or butter
⅓ cup shelled, chopped pistachios
2 T. honey
2 T. lemon juice
1 or 2 T. water
salt, pepper to taste
dash of cinnamon

In a small skillet, heat oil and sauté pistachios for 3 to 5 minutes until lightly browned. Add honey, lemon juice, water and seasonings. Stir well to heat throughout. Toss steamed carrots with sautéed nuts until thoroughly coated. Serve hot.

RICH VEGETARIAN GRAVY

*This rich gravy is delicious over tofu or tempeh cutlets,
rice or potatoes. Makes a flavourful base for a stew
of chunky vegetables.*

SERVES 4

1 T. sunflower oil
2 cloves garlic, minced
¼ cup tamari
¼ cup flour
½ cup nutritional yeast (not yeast
   for baking - see p. 219)
¼ cup tahini (sesame butter) or
   almond butter
1 T. marjoram
salt, pepper to taste

Heat the oil in a saucepan and
sauté the garlic for 2 minutes.
Stir in the tamari, flour, yeast,
tahini, and marjoram; whisk to
form a smooth paste. Simmer
for 5 minutes, stirring often.

2 to 3 cups water
⅓ cup fresh parsley, minced

Whisk in water to thin the
gravy, which will thicken as it
continues to cook. Simmer for
10 minutes over medium heat;
avoid scorching. Stir in the
parsley; taste; adjust the
seasoning. Serve piping hot.

BEANS

There's a wealth of beans to enjoy for their taste, texture, and efficient protein delivery. See p. 47 to 49 for more information on many varieties of beans. In this section we'll focus on one of the quickest-cooking beans, the versatile aduki bean from Japan.

Adukis (or adzukis, as they are sometimes called) are small, mild red beans grown in Japan. Sold in bulk or packaged in the Oriental section at natural foods stores, adukis are each about the size of a kernel of corn. Their pleasant taste and quick cooking time make them indispensible, and they're more easily digested than most beans. Adukis may be presented as a side dish, added to soups or salads, mashed into a sandwich spread, or added to noodle dishes to form a complete protein.

COOKING

Bring 3 cups of water to the boil in a 2-quart pot. Sort through 1 cup of beans, discarding mud and any fragments of rock. Rinse the beans thoroughly; drain. Add the rinsed beans to the boiling water and boil for 45 minutes to one hour, until the beans are tender but not mushy. Drain the beans; you may wish to reserve the cooking liquid for soups. Yield: 2 to 2½ cups cooked beans.

STORAGE

The raw beans are best kept in a sealed jar in a cool, dry location. Store the cooked beans in their cooking liquid in a sealed container in the fridge for up to 5 days. Adukis may also be stored for later use in the freezer in airtight plastic containers. Remember to bring the cooked beans back to the boil for 3 minutes before use.

OPTIONS

Once they're cooked and drained, these little red beans make a delightful addtition to green salads. Happily married with ginger and sesame, adukis are particularly successful in Japanese-style dishes. In miso broth, with some vegetables, they make an easy soup (see below). Adukis may be substituted for other beans, such as kidney beans, in soups, chilis or stews. Because of their dark red colour, they make attractive pilafs with rice or couscous. Adukis provide a dense, flavourful layer in vegetarian lasagna.

ADUKI MISO SOUP

A comforting bowlful...

5 cups water
1 cup raw aduki beans
3 cloves garlic, minced
1½ T. minced fresh ginger

Bring water to the boil in a soup pot. Rinse the aduki beans and drop them with garlic and ginger into the boiling water; boil, uncovered, for 30 minutes.

1 sweet potato, peeled and diced
1 medium onion, diced
2 stalks green onion, diced

Add sweet potato and onions; cover; simmer for 15 more minutes, until beans and potato are tender.

2 T. miso
1 packed cup chopped spinach leaves, well rinsed
2 to 3 T. tamari

Using a little hot broth from the soup, dilute the miso in a cup. Then return this broth to the soup. Add spinach and tamari, stirring until just heated throughout. DO NOT BOIL. Serve hot.

ADUKI SANDWICH SPREAD

Spread thickly on rice cakes for a healthy lunch.

YIELD: 1¼ CUPS

1 cup cooked aduki beans
2 T. cooking liquid from beans or
 water
1 T. miso or tahini
1 small clove garlic
3 T. sesame seeds
2 green onions, diced
1 T. tamari
1 T. lemon juice

Mash all ingredients together in a food processor or by hand until thoroughly blended. Keeps in the refrigerator for up to 1 week.

ADUKI SALAD DRESSING

Excellent with mixed greens or to flavour a cold rice salad.

YIELD: 1½ CUPS

½ cup cooked, drained aduki beans
1 small clove garlic
1 T. grated fresh ginger
1 T. sweet rice miso
¼ cup green onions, diced
½ cup plain sesame oil
¼ cup lemon juice
¼ cup water

Combine all ingredients in a blender until thoroughly blended.

COLD NOODLE SALAD WITH ADUKI BEANS

A chilled Oriental noodle salad with the flavour of sesame.

SERVES 4

2 T. toasted sesame oil
2 T. sunflower or other light oil
2 T. rice vinegar
1 t. honey
salt
hot chili oil or cayenne
pinch of nutmeg and powdered ginger
    to taste

Combine oil, rice vinegar and honey with seasonings to taste. Mix well.

6 oz. soba or udon noodles, cooked, drained and cooled
2 cups cooked, drained aduki beans
¼ cup each green onion slices, carrot slivers, snow peas
1 cup shredded Napa cabbage or bok choy
½ cup sesame seeds

Toss noodles, beans and vegetables gently with dressing. Garnish with sesame seeds.

TEMPEH

Another high-protein, low-fat soybean product, tempeh is dense and chewy, with a grainy texture similar to meat, and a distinctive flavour. Tempeh originates in Indonesia, where it's often made at home on a daily basis. Look for it here in natural foods stores, in the freezer section. Sometimes soybeans have been blended with grains or seasonings to produce different flavours. Pre-packaged tempeh entrées, such as tempeh burgers, are also available.

STORAGE
Tempeh comes packaged in thin squares, about 5" across and ½" thick, sealed in plastic and stored in the freezer. Take the frozen tempeh out of the freezer and allow it to thaw in the refrigerator the night before you plan to use it, or steam it in a steamer basket for 20 minutes, turning over once.

COOKING
Tempeh may be sliced into strips or cubes and sautéed, fried, broiled, or baked. It may also be ground, mixed with seasonings, and shaped into patties. If sautéed, broiled or baked, tempeh may first be marinated in tamari, vinaigrette, BBQ sauce or the marinade of your choice.

TEMPEH CROUTONS

A simple, tasty way to add protein to salads.

SERVES 4 TO 6

1 (250 gram) pkg. tempeh, thawed
2 T. oil
2 T. tamari
1 t. oregano
½ t. basil

Mix oil, tamari and herbs. Dice the tempeh into ½" cubes and place in a small bowl. Pour the tamari mixture over cubes. PREHEAT OVEN TO 375° F. When the cubes have marinated for 15 to 20 minutes, drain; place them on a cookie sheet and bake for 15 minutes or until very crispy. Cool; toss with a green salad or float in soup as croutons.

LEMON-BROILED TEMPEH

*Savoury tempeh strips with highlights of lemon
and rosemary...serve over a bed of cooked couscous
or bulghar, with accompanying vegetables. Leftover
strips make a satisfying sandwich.*

SERVES 4

2 (250 gram) pkgs. tempeh, thawed

Using a long serrated knife, slice each square of tempeh in half to form two thin sheets. Cut each sheet into 3 strips.

3 T. olive oil
3 T. tamari
3 T. lemon juice
1 t. rosemary
½ t. dried mustard
pepper to taste

Make the marinade by mixing oil, tamari, lemon juice and seasonings. Spoon half the marinade into a rimmed baking sheet. Lay out the strips of tempeh in the marinade, and spoon the remaining liquid over the strips. Let rest for 30 minutes. PREHEAT THE BROILER UNIT OF OVEN.
Drain the tempeh strips, reserving the marinade. Place the strips under the broiler at a distance of 6 to 8", and broil for 7 minutes on each side. Meanwhile, heat marinade in a small saucepan; pour over the broiled strips. Serve hot.

A GUIDE TO GRAINS AND BEANS

Grains and beans form the foundation of a vegetarian diet, as they provide protein, carbohydrates, fibre, calories, and nutrients. Unrefined grains, such as brown rice, millet, whole wheat, oats, and quinoa, are a good source of dietary fibre, which is useful to the body for digestion and has been clinically proven to reduce the risk of certain forms of cancer. These grains are more nutritious and flavourful than the refined grains (white rice, "white" wheat flour). Beans provide soluble fibre, which allows your body to reduce its cholesterol level.

HOW TO COOK RICE

One cup of raw rice, white or brown, will yield 3 cups of cooked rice. An average serving of cooked rice is ¾ to 1 cup per person.

For each cup of raw rice, bring 2 scant cups of water to a boil in a pot with a closely-fitting lid. Add ½ t. salt if desired. When the water is boiling, add rice and stir. When the water has returned to the boil, reduce heat to a simmer, cover, and LEAVE ALONE. Try to resist the temptation to lift the lid on the pot until the end of the cooking period: about 15 minutes for white rice, and 45 minutes for brown rice. Rice is cooked when the grains are tender and all the water has evaporated from the pot. Before serving, stir with a fork to separate the grains.

Staple food to more than half the world's population, rice originally grew in areas of natural flooding. Humankind eventually learned how to irrigate crop fields, and rice is now cultivated in many parts of the world in the flooded fields known as paddies. Rice is versatile; dozens of species have been developed, with diverse flavours and textures. One special advantage: rice does not seem to trigger allergies, unlike some of the other grains.

White rice is brown rice without the hull (and thus many of the nutrients). Although it cooks in a third of the time, white rice offers less nutrition than brown rice. I do recommend that you learn to cook and enjoy brown rice – it may take a little longer to cook, but it offers much better food value and a chewier, more filling texture, as well as more dietary fibre, which is useful to the body.

Long grain rice: best suited to salads and pilafs, as the grains stay separate and "fluffy" in cooking.

Short grain rice: higher in protein than long grain, has a stickier texture when cooked. A good all-purpose rice, ideal for casseroles and puddings.

Basmati rice: cultivated in India, basmati is aromatic and has a nut-like taste. Brown and white strains are available. Because basmati is so flavourful, it makes a good choice whenever you wish to serve rice simply.

Try Sesame Fried Rice (p. 116), Rajah's Rice (p. 87), and San Francisco-Style, (p. 88). Rice is suggested as a side dish for many of the recipes that follow.

HOW TO COOK WILD RICE

Wild rice is not usually eaten unaccompanied: it has a strong, distinctive flavour which lends well to stuffings and pilafs. Each ½ cup of raw wild rice will yield 1 to 1½ cups cooked. Rinse rice well before cooking.

To cook ½ cup raw wild rice, bring 1½ cups water to the boil in a small pot. When the water is boiling, add the rinsed rice, cover, and lower the heat. Gently boil for about 40 minutes, adding small quantities of water as needed to keep the rice covered. Rice grains will pop open as they cook. When grains are tender, remove from heat. Drain and reserve the excess liquid (excellent as a bsse for soups). Combine the cooked rice with other cooked grains as desired, in a ratio of 1 part wild rice to 3 or 4 parts grain.

Wild rice is actually not a rice at all, but the seed of a wild grass that grows in northern Canada and some northern parts of the United States. Harvesting is expensive: the grain must be gathered by hand, using canoes or boats to collect the rice where it grows in the shallows of lakes. Cultivation is legislated and largely limited to native peoples as a traditional crop. Its robust flavour and dark colour make it a good accent in salads. Stuffed Acorn Squash, p. 146, features wild rice with pecans and apples in a festive holiday dish.

HOW TO COOK BARLEY

Add ½ to 1 cup of well-rinsed barley to salted, boiling vegetable stock or soup broth, and let simmer for 20 to 30 minutes. The barley will soak up liquid, so add more stock as needed.

Unpearled barley (with the husk, bran, and germ still attached) is available in natural foods stores. Light brown in colour, this grain is a popular ingredient in soups and stews as it thickens the broth. (You'll find it in Alphabet Vegetable Soup, page 73.) As long as it sits, barley will continue to absorb liquid and to swell, so use it sparingly, and add more liquid as needed.

HOW TO COOK MILLET

One cup of raw millet yields 3 cups cooked. An average serving of cooked millet is ¾ to 1 cup per person. Rinse millet well before cooking.

For each cup of raw millet, bring 2 cups of water to the boil in a pot. Add ½ t. salt if desired. Stir the rinsed millet into the boiling water. When the water has returned to the boil, reduce heat. Simmer uncovered for 20 to 30 minutes. Millet is cooked when the grains are tender and all the water has evaporated from the pot. Before serving, stir with a fork to separate the grains.

Millet may look like birdseed to you, because that has been its traditional use in North America. But this versatile grain has been the daily staple of millions of people for centuries. Millet is a reliable crop which grows well under adverse conditions. Unfortunately, it is losing ground to rice in many regions of China and Africa, partly because rice is seen to be more "sophisticated". This trend helps no one: rice requires a great deal more water and effort to grow, and incurs a much higher incidence of crop failure. Yet more evidence that development does not always equal progress.

A small, seed-like grain with a mild flavour, millet is a more nearly complete protein than almost any other grain. It's particularly easy to digest and especially appropriate for gluten- and allergy-restricted diets. Millet makes a satisfying side dish, good company for stew, and a superb base for casseroles, it also lends body to soups.

HOW TO COOK BULGHAR

One cup of raw bulghar yields 3 cups cooked. An average serving of cooked bulghar is ¾ to 1 cup per person.

For each cup of dry bulghar, bring 2 scant cups of water to the boil in a pot. Add ½ t. salt if desired. Stir the bulghar into the boiling water. When the water has returned to the boil, reduce heat and simmer for about 15 minutes. Bulghar is cooked when the grains are tender and all the water has evaporated from the pot. Before serving, stir with a fork to separate the grains.

Alternate method: you can cook 1 cup bulghar by simply pouring 2 cups of boiling water over the grain. Stir; cover, let rest for 25 to 30 minutes, until the grain is tender. Drain off the excess water. The bulghar will not be quite as fluffy as when cooked over the stove. This method is helpful if you want the bulghar for use at room temperature, as for tabouli, or if burner space is at a premium, as when camping.

Quick-cooking and nutritious, **bulghar wheat** is processed from whole wheat, which is cracked into small pieces, steamed, and dried. With its light nutty taste and chewy texture, bulghar makes a welcome change from rice as the base for stirfries, or a robust contribution to soups and stews. For a hearty spaghetti sauce with bulghar, see p.148. Or start your day with Fruity Hot Cereal (p. 188).

Probably the best known use of bulghar is **tabouli**, a dish prepared throughout the Middle East. To make tabouli, mix cooked bulghar with generous quantities of fresh minced parsely and diced tomatoes; then season to taste with lavish quantities of minced garlic and lemon juice, a splash of olive oil, salt, and pepper. Serve with pita bread. Perfect for summer meals and picnics.

HOW TO COOK CORN AND CORNMEAL

On the cob: Bring a large pot of water to a rolling boil. Remove the husk and any fibres, called silk, from the ears. (Allow 1 to 2 large ears per person.) Drop into boiling water; cook for 10 to 15 minutes, until kernels are tender. Remove from water, serve immediately with butter and salt.

Cornmeal: To cook into a porridge, bring 2½ cups of water to the boil for every 1 cup of cornmeal. When water is boiling, whisk in cornmeal. Add salt and herbs (oregano, basil, marjoram) if desired. Reduce heat and simmer for 20 to 30 minutes, until cornmeal reaches desired consistency. Stir often and monitor heat level so that the bottom layer does not scorch. When the cornmeal is tender and of the proper consistency, remove it from the burner.

Originally native to the Americas, corn is now grown around the world. We enjoy fresh corn on or off the cob as a cooked vegetable. (Is there a finer pleasure on earth than sinking your teeth into an ear of sweetcorn, just boiled and buttered?) The obligatory cinema treat, popcorn, is a distinct variety of corn. Still another variety is dried and ground into both flour and meal. The flour is used to make tortillas, the staple flatbread of Mexico and Central America, and a dense bread from Portugal. The meal is used to make fritters, puddings, the traditional cornbread, muffins, or "pone" of the American south, or boiled into a porridge which the Italians call polenta. Polenta can appear as a layer in a casserole or as a side dish, or may be left to cool, cut into squares, and fried on both sides. And of course feed corn is raised in huge quantities as a staple feed for livestock.

Whether as kernels or ground meal, corn is traditionally partnered with beans; together they form a complete protein. Frozen corn is worth keeping on hand for a quick and easy way to round out bean soups or grain entrées. Cornbread, tortillas, or polenta served with bean dishes is filling and nutritious.

Check out Summer Fritters, p. 129, Frijole Corn Pie, p. 113, Stew à la Tarragon, p. 119, Cornbread, p. 168, and Sage Corn Muffins, p. 169.

HOW TO COOK QUINOA (pronounced: keen-wah)

One cup of raw quinoa yields 2 ½ cups cooked. An average serving of cooked quinoa is 1 cup per person.

For each cup of dry quinoa, bring 2 cups of water to the boil in a pot. Add ½ t. salt if desired. Rinse quinoa well; drain. When the water is boiling, add quinoa and stir. When the water has returned to the boil, reduce heat and simmer for about 15 minutes. Quinoa is cooked when the grains are tender and all the water has been absorbed. Be careful not to overcook. Before serving, stir with a fork to separate the grains.

A grain cultivated since ancient times in South America, quinoa is now grown for the "health food market" in North America. It offers a proportion of amino acids close to the ideal, a nutty flavour, and appealingly light texture. Popular alone or in combination with other grains in salads, quinoa may also substitute for various grains in recipes calling for a fluffy texture. Try it in Corn & Quinoa Soup. p. 76.

HOW TO COOK COUSCOUS

One cup of dry couscous yields 2 cups cooked. An average serving of cooked couscous is 1 cup per person.

For each cup of dry couscous, bring 2 scant cups of water to the boil in a pot. Add ½ t. salt if desired. Stir the couscous into the boiling water. When the water has returned to the boil, reduce heat and simmer for about 10 minutes. Couscous is cooked when the grains are tender and all the water has been absorbed. Before serving, stir with a fork to separate the grains.

Alternate method: you can cook couscous by drytoasting in a cast iron skillet, or by sautéeing in a little oil in a pot, until the grains are lightly browned. Then pour boiling water over the grains, allowing two parts water to one part couscous. Stir; cover; simmer for 10 to 15 minutes. This browning will give the couscous a richer flavour.

Light, delicate, and delicious, couscous is a wheat product made by grinding, briefly cooking and then drying semolina wheat. Because it has been partially pre-cooked, couscous is very quick to prepare. A North African speciality, the name couscous refers to both the grain itself and the aromatic pilaf in which it is commonly featured. In Algeria and Morocco, cooks use a special pot called a *couscousier* which steams the grain as it cooks meat and vegetables for the accompanying stew. Moroccan Couscous (p. 140), provides a delicious example of the traditional ingredients and spicing. Couscous goes well with Ratatouille (p. 109), or as an accompaniment to the Zesty Sesame-Vegetable Medley (p. 112).

HOW TO COOK OATS

To make a porridge: Boil one cup of water for each serving, add ½ t. salt and ½ cup oatmeal, stirring well. When the water has returned to the boil, reduce heat and simmer, uncovered. "Quick cooking" oatmeal cooks in about 5 minutes. When the oat flakes are tender and have reached the desired consistency, remove from heat, cover and set aside for 2 to 3 minutes. Serve hot.

To toast oats for granola: PREHEAT OVEN TO 350° F. Pour oats into a large roasting pan with high sides. Mix in a few tablespoons of soyflour for protein, if desired, and a few tablespoons of oil and honey, using your hands to toss the oats until they are completely coated. Bake for 15 minutes. Remove from the oven and stir thoroughly. At this point you can add nuts, seeds, cinnamon, and/or vanilla extract. Return to the oven and bake another 15 minutes, until the oats are golden brown. Let cool completely. Add raisins or other chopped dried fruits after granola is cooled.

The whole oat grain is processed by slicing: the size of the slice, or flake, determines how quickly the oat will cook. Individual pouches of "instant" oatmeal may be quick and convenient, but they are often processed with sugar and salt. Read the label!

Oats traditionally are a breakfast cereal, boiled into a porridge and served with butter, milk, sugar, or honey. They add a hearty, chewy texture to breads, muffins, and cookies. (See p. 166, 170.) People who are allergic to wheat can enjoy oat flour in baking: the flakes are easily ground in a blender. Oats enjoyed a sudden resurgence in popularity when it was recently discovered that oat bran helps the body to reduce cholesterol.

HOW TO COOK BEANS

Beans are slow-cooking, anywhere from 45 minutes to 5 hours, depending on the variety of bean. For every cup of dried beans, use 3 cups of water for cooking. The beans will swell as they cook: one cup of raw beans will yield about 2½ cups of cooked beans. All dried beans and peas should first be spread out on a tray and thoroughly sorted to remove any dirt or fragments of rock, and rinsed well to remove dust.

Soaking beans before you cook them makes them cook more quickly and evenly. Sort and rinse the beans, then put them in a pot and cover with water. Leave them in a cool place overnight. Beans will soak up most or all the water, so check them once or twice and add more water as needed. (Some people find soaked beans more digestible if they drain off the soaking water and cover the beans with fresh water before cooking.) When it's time to cook them, add more water if necessary, and bring to the boil. Reduce heat slightly and simmer for the required time, again keeping an eye on the water level. Spices may be added to the beans while boiling so that they absorb flavour, but salt should not be added until the beans are already tender, as salt toughens the skin of the beans and slows cooking . If you have trouble digesting beans, try adding a 4" strip of kombu (a broad, green sea weed) as you cook the beans; this is said to help digestibility. Or try a product like "Bean-o", developed to help this problem, from a natural foods store.

A quicker method of soaking only takes an hour. Sort and rinse the beans; drain; cover with water. Bring beans and water to the boil. Remove from heat and let rest for one hour, then cook as usual.

CONTINUED

- Beans that are not pre-soaked will take longer to cook (though quick-cooking legumes such as lentils or split peas do not need to be soaked first).
- Remove and discard any foam that forms on beans while they are cooking.
- Cooking beans slowly and gently improves their flavour and helps them retain their shape.

Beans and peas are from the family of plants called legumes. They've been a staple of the human diet for centuries, traditionally consumed in the company of grains. As complex carbohydrates, beans provide protein, fibre, vitamins, and minerals, as well as the advantage of long-term storage in their dried form. Is it any wonder that countries where meat is scarce rely on beans as a staple food? These qualities make beans and peas a valuable part of a vegetarian diet, especially as they are also filling, delicious and inexpensive.

Cooking times vary from bean to bean and from recipe to recipe. For bean salads, beans should be slightly undercooked, to retain their shape and avoid disintegration. For soups, casseroles and especially for spreads such as refried beans or hummus, they should be cooked until very tender.

The following are just a few of the multitude available. Experiment to see which you prefer. Beans are listed from quickest to slowest cooking; approximate cooking times are given in parenthesis (for method, see box above).

Split green or yellow peas are usually featured in soups, because they swiftly lose their shape, cooking into a thick broth when tender. They are one of the legumes used to make a hearty, plain Indian classic called dahl. Split peas combine well with curry spices, and also with onion, garlic, bay leaf, sage, parsley, thyme, wine, marjoram, and dried mustard. (Cooking time: 45 minutes; no soaking required.)

Aduki beans are small red beans from Japan. See p. 33 to 36 for more information on adukis, including recipes. (Cooking time: 45 minutes; no soaking required.)

Lentils, red, green and brown are used in Middle Eastern, Eastern European, Mediterranean, and Indian cooking. The tiny red lentils cook in less time than the slightly larger greenish brown ones. Excellent in soups (p. 61 & 70), stews, or salads, such as the Spanish Lentil Salad on p. 135. (Cooking time: 45 minutes to one hour; no soaking required.)

Black-eyed peas, are beloved in the southern states of the U.S.A., as well as in Portugal and the Caribbean. This small white bean, originally from Africa, has a black dot in its center. See p. 135 for suggestions. (Cooking time: 1 to 1½ hours; no soaking required.)

White beans come in several shapes and sizes. Navy beans are small, Great Northern and White Kidney somewhat larger: all make pleasant, filling soups. White beans magically absorb the flavours of maple syrup or BBQ sauce as baked beans. (Cooking time: 2 hours.) (See recipe for Creamy Mushroom Bisque, p.63.)

Black beans, also called turtle beans, are small black beans which cook into an aromatic, purple black broth. Grown in Central and South America, black beans are superb in soups, stews, or mashed. They're featured in Three Bean Chili, p. 141, and Brazilian Peanut Stew, p. 138. (Cooking time: 2 to 2½ hours.)

Pinto beans are a staple of Mexican cuisine, as well as the culinary traditions of the American Southwest. The speckled appearance of the dry bean perhaps reminded frontier cooks of the patchy coats of pinto ponies: hence the name. Pinto beans turn a light reddish-brown when cooked, and they have a rich flavour which combines perfectly with corn tortillas, cheese, and fiery hot sauce. Served as a side dish or in salads (p. 158), cooked into soups (p. 141), or mashed into refried beans, (p. 106). (Cooking time: 2½ to 3 hours.)

Kidney beans, named for their shape, are the dark red beans so popular in three-bean salads, soups, and stews. See p. 119 for Stew à la Tarragon, or p. 113, 158 for other kidney bean recipes. (Cooking time: 2½ to 3 hours.)

Chickpeas, also called garbanzo beans, are slow-cooking and versatile. The distinctive crunch of this round white bean is probably familiar to you from salad bars. Chickpeas make a pleasant curry, the hearty base for minestrone, an earthy, garlicky hummus, or a satisfying entrée: try Mexican Greens with Potatoes and Garbanzos, p. 145. Plenty of reasons to have a couple of cans in the cupboard; or better yet, to cook up a pot on the weekend and freeze some small portions for future use. (Cooking time: 4 hours.)

Soybeans, though very high in protein, are the hardest beans to digest in their whole form and take the longest to cook. They are much easier to prepare and enjoy in their processed forms: tofu, tempeh, miso, and soymilk. (Cooking time: 5 hours.)

VEGETARIAN MENU PLANNING

So how do vegetarians put a meal together?.

It's really not difficult at all. You may have to play around a little, until you find combinations of tastes and textures that appeal to you, or until you feel confident that you know how much food or how many dishes to prepare to feed your family or guests. But don't overextend yourself: most vegetarian food is remarkably satisfying. If you fix two or three dishes, just as you would for a meat-based meal, you'll be fine. No one ever left the table hungry after eating lasagna, for instance, whether it was layered with ground beef or a flavourful spinach purée.

For the most part, your vegetarian meals will consist of either an entrée and side dish, or a combination of soup and salad, or two or three "side dishes" served together. The entrées will probably be based on a bean or a grain or meat substitute such as tofu; soups and side dishes may contain beans or grains, but will usually focus on vegetables. Often you will want to serve a simple grain such as rice or bulghar wheat, or pasta, alongside or under a spicier item.

Start with an appreciation for fresh food. Leaf through this book and make yourself familiar with one or two new ingredients at a time. Incorporate these ingredients into your routine. Once you've learned how to use them simply, try a more complicated recipe. Then branch out to another new conquest (Today, tofu. Tomorrow, the world…)! You'll soon have a repertoire of standards for every day, as well as some ideas for special occasions.

Not quite ready? Take a look at the menu suggestions that follow. Remember that these menus, like the recipes themselves, are certainly not carved in stone. Feel free to play around – substitute one vegetable for another, serve a salad instead of a vegetable. Important things to keep in mind are taste, texture, and colour. How will this meal look on the plate? Choose recipes to provide a balance of textures and a variety of colours, and recipes whose seasonings complement each other. (Check the section on herbs and spices if you need help.)

It is essential to find recipes and menu combinations that appeal to you, that are within your capabilities as a cook, and that will work with your routine. Otherwise changing your diet is something that will remain a good intention. You will have to be flexible, a little adventurous, and persistent, at least when you are starting out as a vegetarian. As with any other important life change, there will be days when you just don't want to be bothered, or when you crave the comfort of the familiar. But your desire to eat well will keep you on track, and meals like the ones suggested below will be your reward.

I've included a few menus for special occasion dinners, whether you're just having a few friends over, or entertaining on a grand scale. Perhaps it's a holiday dinner, and you or one of your guests don't want to share in the customary turkey or ham.

What about those occasions when you'll have both "omnivores" and vegetarians as dinner guests? You'll have to judge your audience, as well as your own feelings, in deciding whether to serve an entirely vegetarian meal. You can always prepare a special entrée for the vegetarian(s) present, making enough for all your guests to sample. More and more people these days have stopped eating meat, must monitor their cholesterol, or suffer from food allergies. So it shows consideration of your guests to ask, when you issue an invitation, if there is anything you should avoid when planning the meal. Similarly, if you're the one invited to dinner and mention up front that you have special needs. Why not offer to bring a dish, one that you know you can eat? Goodwill goes a long way to soothing the waters about food choices.

DINNER SUGGESTIONS

Three Bean Chili, p. 141
Sage Corn Muffins, p. 169
Slaw Salvadoreno, p. 82

~

Aloo Gobi, p. 124
Rajah's Rice, p. 87
Yogurt
Coconut Loaf, p. 172

~

Lemon-Broiled Tempeh, p. 38
San Francisco-Style Rice, p. 88
Tomatoes Parmesan, p. 93

~

Mushroom Tofu Sukiyaki, p. 122
Rice, p. 39
Braised Butternut Squash, p. 101

~

Pasta Carbonara, p. 149
Antipasto, p. 104
Bread Sticks

~

Texas Taco Salad , p. 158
Salsa Picante, p. 208
Fruit with Poppyseed
Dressing, p. 189

~

Cashew Vegetable Stirfry, p. 130
Rice, p. 39
Sesame Cucumbers, p. 94

~

Ratatouille, p. 109 served over
Couscous, p. 44
Green Salad, p. 77

~

Alphabet Vegetable Soup, p. 73
Havarti Cheese Dip, p. 204
Sheila's Sesame Oat Crackers, p. 170

~

Okra Gumbo, p. 120
Cornbread, p. 168
Devilled Cauliflower, p. 103

~

Macaroni Moussaka, p. 143
Tzatziki, p. 203
Cucumber & celery sticks

~

Mediterranean Pilaf, p. 137
Lemon- Braised Carrots, p. 95
Green Salad, p. 77

~

Summer Fritters, p. 129
Spicy Breaded Tomatoes, p. 93
Watermelon or canteloupe wedges

~

Avgolemono, p. 65
Greek Salad, p. 85
Crusty Bread

~

Indonesian Green Beans, p. 99
Carrots & Cauliflower in
Indonesian Coconut Sauce, p. 102
Rice, p. 39

~

Quick Ramen-Vegetable Soup, p. 69
Tri-Colour Pepper Triangles, p. 95

~

Baked Potato Soup, p. 60
Caesar Salad, p. 84

~

Sloppy Sams over
Buns, p. 118
Homefries, p. 186
Steamed Broccoli

~

John's Perfect Potato Salad, p. 83
Corn-on-the-Cob, p. 43
Balsamic Tomatoes, p. 93

~

Creamy Mushroom Bisque, p. 63
Popeye's Favourite Grilled
Cheese Sandwich, p. 161
Pickles, Carrot Sticks

~

Migas, p. 185
Santa Fe Beans, p. 106
Tortillas
Fruit Slushies, p. 190

~

Spicy Broccoli Noodles, p. 128
Braised Butternut Squash, p. 101

~

Spanish Lentil Salad
on a bed of lettuce, p. 135
Pepper & Zucchini Sauté, p. 96

~

Corn & Quinoa Soup, p. 76
Mexican Greens with
Potatoes & Garbanzos, p. 145

~

DINNER PARTY
& HOLIDAY SUGGESTIONS

Avgolemono, p. 65
Stuffed Zucchini, p. 133
Salad, p. 77

~

Butternut Apple Soup, p. 71
Yogurt & Herb Scones, p. 165
Romaine & Pine Nut Salad, p. 79
Morrocan Couscous, p. 140

~

Tempeh Fajitas, p. 110
Santa Fe Beans, p. 106

~

Antipasto, p. 104
Lasagna
Salad, p. 77

~

Acorn Squash Stuffed with Wild
Rice and Pecans, p. 146
Cranberry Relish, p. 206
Brussel Sprouts with Walnut
Dressing p. 105
Banana-Coconut Pie, p. 179

~

Tzimmes, p. 147
Brown & Wild Rice Pilaf, p.91
Cider Carrots, p.97
Pumpkin Gingerbread
with whipped cream, p. 171

~

NOTES ON RECIPES

All recipes serve 4, unless otherwise noted.

I often list possible substitutions at the foot of the page. But just because I don't mention any specific substitution you have in mind, doesn't mean that you can't use it: I invite you to be flexible and creative with these recipes, since that's what makes the fun of cooking.

Remember to adjust the seasoning to suit your own taste, and the cooking time to suit the whims of your particular oven. (My own oven rules with an iron fist).

The ingredients are given in imperial measurements, since cups and tablespoons still seem to be most common for cooking. The chart below lists both metric and imperial equivalents; you'll find it repeated throughout the book.

METRIC/IMPERIAL CONVERSIONS

1 teaspoon (t.) = 5 millilitres (ml)
1 tablespoon (T.) = 15 millilitres (ml)
1 cup = approximately 250 ml
1 ounce (oz.) = approximately 30 grams
2.2 pounds (lbs.) = 1 kilogram
1 inch (") = 2.54 centimetres (cm)

SOUPS, SALADS
& SIDE DISHES

SOUPS

Soup is really such a comfort. Soup is what my mother fed me when I could convince her I was "sick". Sick enough to stay home from school, that is, but not sick enough to need the doctor. I don't know if it was Mom's soup that "cured" me, or just getting to stay home, watch cartoons, and read. Those halcyon days are gone now, and I live in Canada. Soup is what gives me courage to face the wait for a streetcar on a February day.

Soup makes a great centrepiece for vegetarian meals, summer or winter. It can be the hearty kind that sticks to your ribs, or light and lovely to look at, presented in a flat bowl with a garnish. Soup is "convenience food", in a way, because once you've invested the time to make a pot of soup, you can live on it for a week, or freeze leftovers for future meals.

I hope you enjoy the selection of soups that follow, from rich and creamy Baked Potato Soup to light and flavourful Corn & Quinoa. And if you ever feel the need to stay home and watch reruns or curl up with a book, may I suggest Alphabet Vegetable for lunch?

ANDALUSIAN CREAM OF TOMATO SOUP

Delicious, comforting and remarkably easy to make.

SERVES 4

2 T. olive oil
4 cloves garlic, minced
1 cup diced onions
2 cups diced celery
1 (28 oz.) can tomatoes
salt, pepper to taste
1 T. dried marjoram
1 t. dried sage or tarragon
1 bay leaf

Heat oil in heavy-bottomed soup pot. Sauté onions, celery, and garlic over medium heat for 5 minutes. Drain tomatoes, reserving juice. Chop canned tomatoes coarsely and add to the pot. Season to taste. Simmer for 20 minutes, stirring often.

juice from canned tomatoes
1 cup water
1 cup cooked rice (optional)
¼ cup minced fresh parsley
1 cup cream or milk or soymilk

Add tomato juice, water, cooked rice and parsley to the soup. Heat thoroughly over medium heat. Add cream and heat gently, stirring often. DO NOT BOIL: avoid scorching. Serve steaming hot, in warmed bowls, with garlic bread.

BAKED POTATO SOUP

A hearty, creamy excuse to enjoy your favourite baked potato toppings.

8 cups water
4 large potatoes, peeled and cubed
2 t. salt
1 bay leaf

Bring water to a rolling boil in a 4-quart pot. Add potatoes, salt, and bay leaf; return to the boil. Reduce heat to medium and simmer, uncovered, for 15 minutes or until potatoes are tender. Drain, reserving 2 cups of the cooking water. Discard bay leaf.

3 T. oil or butter
2 cups sliced leeks or onions
2 or 3 cloves garlic, minced
1 T. paprika
1 t. black pepper

Heat oil in a skillet. Sauté onion and garlic with seasonings until soft.

1 cup sour cream or yogurt
1 cup grated cheddar cheese

In a blender or food processor, blend the potatoes and onions together with sour cream and cheese. Pour in small quantities of the reserved cooking water, a few tablespoons at a time, until the soup has the desired consistency.

1 bunch green onions, diced
3 T. fresh minced parsley, dill or tarragon (optional)

Return the soup to the pot and stir in the green onions (and herbs). Heat gently. DO NOT BOIL. Serve piping hot. Garnish each serving with diced chive or green onions, or a dash of paprika.

BENJAMIN'S LENTIL SOUP

*My friend Gladys Amaya makes this soothing
El Salvadorean soup for her son, Benjamin.*

SERVES 4

6 cups water or vegetable stock
2 cups brown lentils
2 t. salt (optional)
1 bay leaf

Rinse lentils thoroughly; drain.
Bring water to the boil in a
heavy soup pot. Add lentils,
bay leaf (and salt). Reduce heat
and simmer for 45 minutes, until
lentils are tender.

3 T. olive oil
1 medium onion, diced
4 cloves garlic, minced
4 stalks celery, diced
2 medium carrots, diced
1 cup diced cabbage
2 T. ground cumin
1 T. oregano
salt, pepper to taste

While lentils are simmering,
heat oil in a skillet. Sauté the
vegetables and seasonings until
onions are golden. Add to the
lentils for the final 20 minutes
of cooking. Stir well; adjust
seasoning to taste. Serve hot.

VEGETABLE CHOWDER

*Seasonal vegetables in a milky broth. Enjoy it with
Yogurt & Herb Scones (p. 165) or a Caesar Salad (p. 84).*

SERVES 4

2 T. oil or butter
2 medium potatoes, diced
2 medium carrots, diced
2 stalks celery, diced
salt, pepper to taste
¼ cup vegetable stock or white wine

Heat oil in a heavy soup pot with a lid. Add the vegetables and liquid; cover. Simmer over medium heat, stirring occasionally, for 20 minutes until just tender.

1 cup sliced mushrooms
1 bunch green onions, diced
1 cup frozen corn
1 cup frozen peas
¼ cup parsley, minced
¼ cup celery leaves, minced
3 T. fresh basil or marjoram
    (or 1 T. dried)
1 cup cooked navy or aduki beans
    (optional)

Add the mushrooms, cover and simmer for 5 more minutes. Add the other vegetables, herbs (and beans). Stir well, simmering until all the vegetables are tender.

3 cups milk or soymilk

Add to pot. Stir well, simmering until heated throughout. Reduce heat as needed. DO NOT BOIL! Taste and adjust seasonings. Serve hot.

Turnip or sweet potato make pleasant variations: add during the initial cooking period. Add lightly steamed asparagus, broccoli florets, or diced zucchini in addition to or instead of the mushrooms. The beans give the soup more body; one cup of cooked, small-shaped pasta is also welcome. Almost any fresh herb works well. This soup takes wonderful advantage of whatever's available, in the market or in your fridge.

CREAMY MUSHROOM BISQUE

The delicate flavour of mushrooms, the velvety texture of blended navy beans. Not as rich as a cream-based soup, and just as delicious.

6 cups water or vegetable stock
2 cups dried navy beans (or any white bean)
2 cloves garlic, diced
1 medium onion, diced
1 bay leaf

Bring water to the boil in a heavy-bottomed soup pot. Sort and rinse beans to remove any impurities. Add beans and seasonings to the pot. Once water has returned to the boil, reduce heat to a gentle simmer. Cook for 2 hours, or until beans are completely tender. Add water or stock as needed to keep beans barely covered. Remove bay leaf.

4 T. oil or butter
1 medium onion, diced
1 pound mushrooms (white, brown or a mixture), cleaned and sliced
salt, white pepper to taste
4 T. lemon juice or white wine

Sauté onions in oil over medium heat until tender, but not browned. Add mushrooms and seasonings; cover. Simmer, stirring, for 10 minutes, or until mushrooms are very limp. Add to the beans in soup pot.

Optional (but recommended):
1/3 to 1/2 cup dried mushrooms (shiitakes or porcini or other)
1 cup water

Rinse dried mushrooms well. Cover with water and boil for 10 minutes. Remove from heat and cool for 20 minutes. Drain, reserving liquid. Mince the reconstituted mushrooms and add to the soup. Strain the cooking liquid and add to the soup.

CONTINUED

Allow the soup to cool before blending. Drain, reserving the cooking liquid. Blend beans and mushrooms together in a blender or food processor until smooth and completely blended. Add as much of the cooking liquid as necessary to obtain the desired consistency. Return to the pot, and warm gently. Stir to prevent scorching. Serve hot.

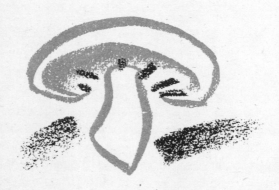

AVGOLEMONO

*This lemony Greek ambrosia is enriched with
beaten egg. Serve with crusty bread
and a fresh tomato salad.*

6 cups vegetable stock
4 T. chicken-flavour vegetable
    bouillon (optional)
1 cup rice
½ cup fresh parsley, minced
salt, pepper to taste

2 small eggs
juice and minced zest of 2 to 3 lemons
1 T. cold water

Bring the stock (and bouillon) to a boil in a soup pot. Add the rice, reduce the heat and simmer for 20 minutes. Add parsley; season to taste with salt and pepper.

In a mixing bowl, beat the eggs until frothy; stir in the lemon juice and water. Remove the soup from the heat. Slowly whisk a ladleful of hot soup into the beaten egg. Add another ladleful or two of hot soup, then pour the warmed egg mixture into the soup pot. Stir well. Garnish with paper-thin slices of lemon, and serve at once.

If you must keep the soup warm on the stove, keep it over very low heat. DO NOT LET THE SOUP BOIL after the eggs have been incorporated, or it will curdle.

CONTINUED

A light soup with few ingredients, such as this one, relies on the broth for flavour. Be sure to use a vegetable stock with a full-bodied but pleasant taste (i.e., one that doesn't taste too strongly of cabbage, etc.). See p. 195 to make your own vegetable stock.

Instant vegetable bouillon, in powder or cube form, is available at natural foods stores. A mixture of dehydrated vegetables and herbs which gives a rich, salty taste to soup broths, this bouillon is handy for those occasions when you don't have stock on hand. (There's even a vegetarian version of "chicken-flavour" bouillon, made with nutritional yeast – it has a remarkably familiar flavour!) Read the label carefully to make sure you are buying a vegetarian product.

SOUTHWESTERN ROASTED RED PEPPER PURÉE

The gorgeous colour and characteristic smoky flavour of roasted red peppers. Serve this fragrant purée with Mexican Greens with Potatoes (p. 145), and Cornbread (p. 168) or tortillas.

SERVES 4

4 medium red bell peppers
2 large cloves garlic

Roast the peppers with the garlic; cool and peel. (See directions in box below). Chop the peppers; purée with the roasted garlic in a blender or food processor until very smooth. Set aside.

3 T. butter
3 T. flour
4 cups vegetable stock (or chicken-flavour bouillon dissolved in 4 cups boiling water)
salt, pepper to taste

Melt the butter in a soup pot. Whisk in the flour, and cook for several minutes until the roux (the flour and butter mixture) is lightly browned. Still whisking, gradually pour the stock into the roux. Season; bring to the boil. Reduce heat and simmer for 5 minutes, stirring occasionally. Add the purée of peppers and simmer another 5 minutes, stirring.

¼ cup sour cream
1 cup cooked rice
½ cup minced fresh parsley
3 T. minced fresh sage or 1 (4 oz.) can roasted green chilis (or both)

Stir remaining ingredients into soup. Simmer until heated throughout. Serve warm in flat bowls, garnished with parsley or a small spoonful of sour cream.

CONTINUED

HOW TO ROAST RED PEPPERS:

PREHEAT OVEN TO 450° F. Cut off the tops of the peppers and remove all the seeds and membranes. Cut the garlic cloves in half, and tuck one half inside each pepper. Place peppers on a rimmed baking sheet and roast for 15 to 20 minutes, turning them occasionally until they are very dark and blistered on the outside. (You can also roast them directly over the flame on a gas range, using tongs to safely hold the peppers. Or blacken them over the coals on a grill outside.) Remove from the oven and cover with a damp towel (or place in a paper bag); cool. When cool enough to handle, peel and discard all the blackened skin. Cut the peppers into strips to use in salads, or dice to accent casseroles or pasta dishes. Try leaving the peppers whole, served in olive oil as a lovely highlight to Italian meals (see p. 96).

QUICK RAMEN-VEGETABLE SOUP

*A very fast meal-in-a-bowl that features the vegetables
you have on hand. Curly ramen noodles make it filling,
and it's ready in just over 20 minutes.*

SERVES 4

4 cups water or vegetable stock
1 pkg. ramen noodles

Bring water to the boil in soup pot. Break up ramen noodles or drop whole into boiling water. Boil 12 to 15 minutes until noodles are tender. Stir occasionally with a fork to separate noodles.

3 cups of diced vegetables (choose
    from onion, carrot, celery, snow
    peas, corn, mushrooms, peppers,
    cabbage, broccoli)
1 clove garlic, minced
3 T. toasted sesame oil
½ t. dried ginger
½ t. nutmeg

While noodles are boiling, dice up vegetables. Heat oil in a wok. Add vegetables and seasonings. Stirfry 3 to 5 minutes. Add stirfried vegetables to noodles and simmer for 5 more minutes.

4 T. tamari
1 T. mirin or saki (optional)

Stir in the tamari (and mirin). Adjust seasonings to taste. Serve hot.

EASTERN EUROPEAN LENTIL SOUP

Marjoram, dill and lentils are common companions
in Eastern European cooking.

SERVES 4

6 cups water or vegetable stock
1½ cups brown lentils
1 bay leaf
2 medium potatoes, peeled and diced
1 t. salt

Rinse lentils well; drain. Bring water to the boil in a heavy soup pot. Add lentils, bay leaf. Reduce heat and simmer for 20 minutes. Add potatoes and salt, simmering for another 20 to 25 minutes, or until the lentils and potatoes are tender.

3 T. oil
1 medium onion, diced
2 cloves garlic, minced
2 medium tomatoes, diced
1 cup sliced mushrooms
2 T. marjoram
2 T. minced fresh dill
1 or 2 T. wine vinegar
salt, pepper to taste

While lentils are simmering, heat oil in a skillet. Sauté the vegetables with seasonings until onions are tender. Add to the lentils for the final 10 minutes of cooking. Stir well; adjust seasoning to taste. Serve hot, with a dark rye or pumpernickel bread, and some good cheese.

BUTTERNUT APPLE SOUP

*An elegant opener for dinner parties, this pale orange purée
has tantalizing highlights of apple and nutmeg. Make it
in the fall, when apples and squash are plentiful.*

SERVES 4

2 lbs. squash (butternut or acorn),
peeled and cooked

Prepare squash and set aside.
(See box for directions.)

2 T. oil
2 medium onions, diced
2 cloves garlic, minced
½ t. nutmeg
salt, pepper to taste
dash of cayenne
dash of cinnamon
1 Granny Smith apple, peeled and
diced
½ cup water

Heat oil in a soup pot. Sauté
onion with garlic and
seasonings over medium heat
for 10 minutes, until onion is
transparent. Add diced apple
and water; sauté for several
minutes.

3 T. flour
1 cup water

Dust onions with flour, stirring
until flour is dissolved. Add 1 cup
water; stir well. Simmer for 5
minutes; remove from heat and
cool.

water or milk as needed
minced parsley as garnish

Put equal amounts of peeled,
cooked squash and onion mixture
into a blender or food processor:
blend in two batches. Purée until
smooth, adding more water or
milk to obtain the desired consistency. Return the soup to the pot
and heat gently; stir to avoid
scorching. DO NOT BOIL. Garnish
each serving with a snippet of
parsley and serve hot. (Leftovers
are especially good with gruyère
cheese on toasted english muffins.)

CONTINUED

TO COOK SQUASH:

PREHEAT OVEN TO 375° F. Cut squash in half; scrape out seeds and fibres. Then place cut side down on an oiled tray, and bake for 20 to 30 minutes until tender through to the skin. Cool. Scrape out cooked squash and discard the skin.

OR

Cut squash into wedges for easier handling. Peel carefully, using a sharp knife. Remove seeds and fibres. Cube the peeled squash and boil for 15 to 20 minutes until tender, then drain. Reserve the cooking liquid for soup.

ALPHABET VEGETABLE SOUP

A great lunch for kids of all ages! Take some to school or work in a Thermos. Particularly good with a grilled cheese sandwich.

SERVES 4

3 cups water
¼ cup barley
2 large potatoes, finely diced
2 large carrots, peeled and finely diced
2 stalks celery, finely diced
1 medium onion, finely diced
1 cup pasta (alphabet-shapes or small bowties or macaroni)
1 T. marjoram
2 T. tamari
1 bay leaf

Put water, vegetables, barley, and seasonings in a large soup pot with a lid. Bring to the boil. Reduce heat and simmer, covered, for 15 minutes. Add pasta; simmer another 15 minutes, until vegetables and pasta are tender.

3 cups tomato juice
1 zucchini, finely diced
1 cup sliced mushrooms
½ cup frozen peas
½ cup frozen corn kernels
½ cup fresh parsley, minced
salt, pepper to taste

Add tomato juice and remaining vegetables to the soup. Simmer, uncovered, over medium heat, for 15 minutes. Serve hot, with or without a dictionary.

JAPANESE COUNTRY-STYLE SOUP

*Chunks of hearty vegetables swimming in a mild broth make this soup
healthful and energizing. Treat your body to a bowlful when you've had a
hard day or if you feel a cold coming on; you'll feel better.*

SERVES 4

6 cups vegetable stock
1 leek, sliced
2 cups chopped daikon radish
2 cups chopped sweet potato or winter
   squash
1 cup sliced carrots
1 block tofu, cut into ¾" cubes
1" fresh ginger, minced
2 cloves garlic, minced

Bring stock to the boil in a large
soup pot. Add vegetables, tofu,
garlic, and ginger. When the
stock has returned to the boil,
reduce heat and simmer,
covered, for 15 minutes.

1 cup corn kernels or snow peas
1 cup broccoli florets
1 bunch green onions, diced

Drop vegetables into the soup
and simmer another 5 minutes,
or until all the vegetables are
tender.

3 to 4 T. miso

Ladle ½ cup broth from the pot
into a bowl. Stir miso into
reserved broth until dissolved.
Return to soup; stir well and
remove from heat. (Do not
allow soup to boil again after
miso has been added.) Serve
immediately. This soup keeps
well in the fridge for 3 to 4
days; the flavour improves with
time.

CONTINUED

Soup is not an exact science. There's no need to measure vegetables precisely, or to conform rigidly to the ones listed here. My friend Dann McCann creates endless variations of this soup with produce in season, especially root vegetables. For stock he uses the cooking water from steamed vegetables, drained and kept in a jar in the refrigerator.

Variations: Rinse and chop a piece of kombu (a sea vegetable) into 1" lengths; drop it into the pot to simmer with the other vegetables. Add or substitute turnip or parsnip, thinly sliced burdock root, or sliced shiitake mushrooms.

In the final minutes of cooking, stir in 1 cup cooked millet or cooked aduki beans. Add 1 or 2 T. of tamari or toasted sesame oil for flavour.

CORN & QUINOA SOUP

Lemon, coriander, and cinnamon give a warm, bright note to this high-protein soup. Slip sliced avocado into the soup bowls just before serving, and pass a basket of tortilla chips.

SERVES 4

2 T. oil
1 large leek, diced and well-rinsed (or
   1 red onion, diced)
3 cloves garlic, minced
1" piece of cinnamon stick
1 t. ground coriander
1 bay leaf
1 cup diced zucchini

Heat oil in a soup pot. Sauté leek, garlic, and seasonings for 15 minutes, until the leek is tender. Add zucchini; sauté another 5 minutes.

6 cups vegetable stock
1 cup quinoa
1 bunch green onions, diced
1 cup corn kernels
⅓ cup lemon juice
⅓ cup fresh parsley, or cilantro,
   minced
salt, pepper to taste

Add vegetable stock to the pot. Bring to the boil. Stir in the quinoa, reducing heat slightly. Simmer for 15 to 20 minutes until the grain is tender. Add green onions, corn, lemon, and parsley, stirring well. Cook for another 5 minutes. Remove cinnamon stick and bay leaf. Taste and adjust seasoning. Serve hot.

SALADS

The expression "salad days" means the time of youth and inexperience.
Well, we can't buy a return ticket to youth and inexperience – and some of
us wouldn't want to! But we can put a little bounce back into our step, and
evoke a memory of Spring in the depths of Winter. Salads are a wonderful
way to refresh a jaded palate and cut down on calories, all at the same time.
An artfully composed salad is a still life on the plate, a chance to showcase
whatever's fresh from the garden or market. Salads today provide an
excellent source of low-calorie, insoluble fibre and vitamins. They're a far
cry from the iceberg lettuce I grew up with: grains, steamed vegetables, fresh
herbs, and even edible flowers make the contemporary salad versatile and
nutritious.

Toss caution to the wind, and toss up a salad for lunch or
dinner. Throw in a handful of:

alfalfa sprouts	nasturtium petals
apple chunks	nuts
avocado wedges	orange sections, peeled
beans, cooked and drained	olives
carrots, grated	pasta
chick peas	peppers, fresh or roasted
cilantro	raisins
corn kernels	red cabbage, thinly shredded
daikon radish, grated	rice
fresh basil or dill, minced	snow peas
green onions	sunflower seeds
green beans	sunflower sprouts
hard-boiled egg, sliced	tempeh croutons
jicama, julienned	tofu cubes
kale	watercress

And if your salad supplies flavour, crunch, and freshness, there's no need to drown it in dressing. The commercial dressings may be convenient, but they're also expensive, high in calories, and full of preservatives. A scant drizzle of good olive oil, a tablespoon of balsamic vinegar, and a generous grind of fresh black pepper provide the best kind of benediction for an authentic salad. If you wish, a squeeze of lemon juice, and a sprinkle of walnut or sesame oil may take the place of a heavier dressing. Experiment with your own fresh combinations, or see p. 79, 85, and 189.

ROMAINE AND PINE NUT SALAD
WITH CITRUS DRESSING

*A good salad combines a pleasing mix of flavours and textures with
a refreshing dressing. Spinach leaves make an
attractive substitute for the romaine.*

SERVES 4

1 clove garlic, minced
zest and juice of 2 oranges or
    tangerines
¼ cup fresh minced parsley
1 to 2 T. balsamic vinegar
⅔ cup sunflower oil
salt, pepper to taste

Blend garlic, orange zest and
juice, parsley, and vinegar.
While blending or whisking,
pour in the oil in a slow stream.
Taste; adjust seasoning. Set
aside.

1 large head romaine lettuce, rinsed
    and torn into small pieces
1 cup grated carrot
½ cup toasted pine nuts
1 cup cucumber slices
½ cup raisins

Toss vegetables and pine nuts
together in a decorative salad
bowl. Pass the dressing
separately, or toss immediately
before serving.

WALDORF SALAD

*Combine yogurt with mayonnaise for a lighter version
of the famous apple and celery salad. Good company
with low-fat cottage cheese as a light summer meal.*

SERVES 4

4 medium apples, chopped
(Granny Smith and/or Red
    Delicious)
3 stalks celery, chopped
½ cup walnuts, toasted
½ cup sunflower seeds
4 T. lemon juice
zest of one lemon
½ cup Gouda cheese, cubed
    (optional)

Toss apples, celery, nuts and
seeds (and cheese) in a salad
bowl with lemon juice and zest.

½ cup mayonnaise
½ cup low-fat yogurt
½ t. nutmeg
½ t. dried mustard
1 t. honey
salt, white pepper to taste

Blend dressing ingredients
together. Combine gently but
thoroughly with apples. Chill. If
desired, present on lettuce-lined
salad plates. Garnish with mint
sprigs or celery leaves.

CRISP VEGETABLE SALAD

*A fast, cool, summer favourite, this salad is also a
reliable winter pick-me-up when your taste buds
cry out for crisp and fresh.*

SERVES 4

2 large carrots, peeled and julienned
½ English cucumber, julienned
1 red or yellow pepper, julienned
1 bunch watercress, rinsed and
　　trimmed (optional)
2 T. sunflower oil
2 T. balsamic or wine vinegar
½ t. dried dill
salt, pepper to taste

Place the cut vegetables in a
serving bowl. Add oil, vinegar,
and seasonings. Toss gently
with a fork until thoroughly
coated. Let stand in fridge for
30 minutes to develop flavours.

CZECH SALAD

*A pleasant salad from Czechoslovakia. Best in late summer,
when tomatoes are at their peak.*

SERVES 4

1 English cucumber
2 large tomatoes
6 to 8 red radishes

Rinse and finely dice the
vegetables. Place in a serving
bowl.

2 T. hot water
2 t. honey
3 T. apple cider vinegar
salt, pepper to taste

Dissolve the honey in hot
water. Whisk in the vinegar. Stir
the dressing into the diced
vegetables, tossing gently and
thoroughly. Season to taste.
Cover and chill in the fridge for
30 minutes, or serve at room
temperature.

SLAW SALVADORENO

A cumin seed and oregano vinaigrette invigorates this
cabbage salad from El Salvador.

SERVES 4

3 cups shredded cabbage
1 cup grated carrot
½ cup slivered red onion
¼ cup fresh parsley, minced

Toss vegetables together in a salad bowl.

¼ cup apple cider vinegar
1 ½ T. oregano
2 t. cumin seeds
sprinkle of dried hot chilis, crumbled
salt, pepper to taste
½ cup good quality olive oil

Mix vinegar with seasonings. While whisking, trickle in the oil in a steady stream. Pour over the prepared vegetables. Set aside for 20 minutes to develop flavours.

METRIC/IMPERIAL CONVERSIONS

1 teaspoon (t.) = 5 millilitres (ml)
1 tablespoon (T.) = 15 millilitres (ml)
1 cup = approximately 250 ml
1 ounce (oz.) = approximately 30 grams
2.2 pounds (lbs.) = 1 kilogram
1 inch (") = 2.54 centimetres (cm)

JOHN'S PERFECT POTATO SALAD

This potato salad is so good I always want to keep on eating, serving after serving. It tastes even better the next day, so if you practice restraint and have leftovers, take them to work for a brown bag treat. But be forewarned: this potato salad is so good, you may find yourself eating it straight out of the container, standing in front of the fridge at 3 a.m., without even knowing how you got there.

SERVES 4

2 lbs. potatoes, whole
(about 6 medium potatoes)

Scrub potatoes. Place whole and unpeeled in a pot; cover with water. Bring to the boil over high heat. Simmer until just tender, but cooked throughout. Drain; rinse in cold water to cool. Peel and cut potatoes into small cubes. Set aside in a large mixing bowl.

1 cup diced carrots
1 cup frozen peas

Place carrots in a pot; cover with water. Bring to a boil; simmer until the carrots are just tender, about 5 minutes. Remove from heat. Stir in peas, until thawed. Drain; add to cooked potatoes.

½ cup minced dill pickles (about 2 medium pickles)
3 T. capers, minced
1 cup mayonnaise or tofumayo
3 T. dijon mustard
2 T. lemon juice
2 t. dried tarragon
⅓ cup fresh parsley, minced
salt, pepper to taste
2 hard-boiled eggs, chopped (optional)

Combine minced pickles and remaining ingredients in a small bowl. Add to potatoes; toss gently until potatoes are thoroughly coated with the dressing. Serve at room temperature. (This is a mayonnaise-based salad, so you will need to keep it refrigerated. Remember not to leave it out for any length of time in warm weather.)

CAESAR SALAD

A Caesar salad makes a summer dinner in itself,
especially when served with high-protein tempeh croutons.
In winter, precede with a steaming bowl of soup.

1 large head romaine lettuce
1 red onion, chopped

Rinse and dry the lettuce well. Tear it into manageable pieces, and toss with onion in a large salad bowl (large enough to toss the salad vigorously).

1 egg
2 to 3 cloves garlic, minced
½ t. dried mustard
1 t. salt
black pepper, to taste
1 T. capers, minced
2 T. lemon juice or wine vinegar
a few drops of Tabasco and
    Worchestershire
½ cup olive oil
½ cup parmesan cheese

Blend egg, garlic, and seasonings in a blender, or whisk together in a bowl. While blending or whisking, trickle in the oil in a steady stream, until the dressing emulsifies. Pour over lettuce, add parmesan, and toss well. Serve immediately, with lots of tempeh croutons (see p. 37), or bread croutons.

GREEK SALAD

Perfect with Tzatziki (p. 203) and a crusty bread.
An evocative meal in the dead of winter, or
whenever you're dreaming of sun-drenched
beaches and azure seas.

SERVES 4

1 large head lettuce (green leaf or romaine), shredded
2 tomatoes, cut in wedges
½ English cucumber, diced
½ red onion, diced (optional)
½ cup black Calamata olives
4 oz. feta cheese, crumbled

Nest shredded lettuce evenly on 4 salad plates. Arrange tomatoes, cucumber, onion, and olives attractively over the lettuce. Top with feta.

5 T. good quality olive oil
2 T. wine vinegar or lemon juice
1 t. oregano
½ t. marjoram
salt, pepper to taste

Whisk dressing ingredients vigorously together. Drizzle over prepared salad plates. Serve immediately.

GRAINS

Grains are an essential part of a vegetarian diet. Cooked and served very simply, grains such as rice, millet, couscous, or bulghar wheat are comforting, satisfying, and filling. They round out a meal or form a sturdy base for sautées, stews, and stir fries. Combined with herbs, spices, and vegetables, grains provide savour and sustenance as pilafs or side dishes. See pages 39 to 46 for information on grains and how to cook them.

RAJAH'S RICE

This aromatic presentation brings out the inherent excellence of basmati rice, adding exotic hints of cardamom and saffron. Superb with any Indian dish.

SERVES 4

2 cups water
1 ¼ cups white or brown basmati rice
1 bay leaf
5 cardamom pods
½ t. salt
pinch of saffron

Bring water to the boil in a pot with a closely-fitting lid. Add rice and seasonings. When the water has returned to the boil, reduce heat and cover. Simmer for 15 to 20 minutes (45 for brown basmati), or until rice is tender and all water has been absorbed. Remove bay leaf and cardamom pods. Serve hot.

SAN FRANCISCO-STYLE RICE

A tasty rice and pasta pilaf.

SERVES 4

2 T. olive oil
1 ¼ cups brown rice
2 oz. spaghetti, broken into ½ to ¾"
    lengths
3 cloves garlic, minced
1 t. salt
¾ t. pepper
½ t. tumeric

Heat oil in a 2 quart pot with a closely-fitting lid. Sauté rice pasta, garlic, and seasonings together, uncovered, over medium high heat. Stir constantly, until rice is lightly browned.

3 cups boiling water
1 bay leaf
1 cube vegetable bouillon (or 1
    T. vegetable stock powder)
1 T. marjoram
½ cup fresh parsley, minced
¼ cup lemon juice
2 T. butter

Pour boiling water into the browned rice with caution: a great rush of steam will erupt. Stir in the bouillon and marjoram. Reduce heat to low; cover. Simmer for 40 minutes, or until rice is tender. When rice is fluffy, remove the pot from the heat and stir in parsley, lemon juice, and butter. Cover and let rest for 5 minutes. Serve hot.

Regular or spinach spaghetti, tiny bowties, or the small, rice-shaped noodles called orso, make excellent pasta choices for this recipe.

SOUTH AMERICAN RICE

A colourful and fragrant side dish that goes well with Brazilian Peanut Stew(p. 138). These flavours also complement Lemon- Broiled Tempeh (p. 38), as well as Indonesian and Thai dishes.

SERVES 4

2 T. oil
1 medium onion, finely diced
½ red bell pepper, finely diced
½ green bell pepper, finely diced
1 small fresh hot chili, seeded and
    diced (or chili oil, or dried
    chilis to taste)
2 t. salt
1 cup rice

Heat oil in a pot wit a closely-fitting lid. Sauté onions, peppers, and seasonings until tender but not brown. Add rice and sauté an additional 4 to 5 minutes, without browning.

1 cup canned coconut milk
1 cup water

⅓ cup lemon juice
½ cup fresh cilantro, minced
salt, pepper to taste

Add coconut milk and water to rice. Cook over medium high heat until the liquid boils. Reduce heat; cover. Simmer (20 minutes for white rice, 45 minutes for brown) until rice is tender. Stir in cilantro and lemon juice. Taste and adjust seasoning. Remove from heat and let rest, covered, for several minutes. Serve immediately.

CUMIN AND CORN PILAF

Cumin and chili powder bring Mexican sizzle to this flavourful pilaf of bulghar wheat and corn. Pair it up with a Texas Taco Salad, p. 158.

SERVES 4

2 T. corn oil
1 medium onion, diced
2 cloves garlic, minced
1 medium red bell pepper, seeded and
   diced
1 T. chili powder
1 t. cumin
salt, pepper to taste
1 cup bulghar wheat

Heat oil in a pot with a lid. Sauté the onion, garlic, peppers, and seasonings until barely tender. Add bulghar wheat. Cook, stirring, until golden brown.

2 cups boiling water

Pour boiling water over the bulghar. Cover. Reduce heat and simmer for 10 to 15 minutes until water is absorbed and bulghar is tender.

1 ½ cups corn kernels
½ cup fresh parsley or cilantro,
   minced
⅓ cup lemon or lime juice

Add corn, parsley, and lemon juice to the cooked bulghar. Stir briskly until thoroughly mixed. Remove from heat and let rest, covered, for several minutes. Serve piping hot.

BROWN & WILD RICE PILAF

An elegant salad of brown and wild rice, accented by the tastes of orange and fresh mint. Serve with baked squash and a green salad.

SERVES 4

2 cups water
1 t. salt
1 cup long grain brown rice

Bring salted water to a boil, and stir in rice. When the water has returned to a boil, reduce heat to low. Simmer, covered, for 45 minutes until rice is tender and the water has been absorbed. Spread out the rice in a large mixing bowl to cool.

2 cups water
½ cup wild rice

In a separate small pot, bring water to a boil. Stir in wild rice, and reduce the heat slightly. Cook uncovered for 15 to 20 minutes until tender. Drain off excess water. Add wild rice to cooked brown rice to cool

½ cup pecans or walnuts or pine nuts, toasted and chopped
¼ cup raisins
2 T. good quality olive oil
zest and juice of 1 large orange
1 T. tamari
3 cloves garlic, minced
¼ cup fresh mint, minced
¼ cup fresh parsley, minced
4 green onions, diced
1 t. nutmeg
black pepper to taste

Mix nuts and remaining ingredients together. Stir into cooled rice until thoroughly blended. Serve at room temperature. (Leftovers are great to take to work.)

VEGETABLES

I revel in farmer's markets, in the shapes and colours of fresh produce. Asparagus whispers my name tenderly in the early spring. The fragrance of fresh dill can make me swoon. Show me a molehill of pumpkins and I dream of a mountain of pumpkin pies. I get a little giddy, and always end up taking home more than I can possibly eat. Even a well-stocked produce department in a grocery store can set me scheming.

But it wasn't always that way. As a child, my vegetable choices were potatoes, and potatoes. I could be persuaded to eat broccoli, green beans sometimes, and carrots if my mom put sugar on them. Oh, and corn-on-the-cob, of course, but that was more like Having Fun than Eating Vegetables. The list of vegetables I wouldn't touch was longer than my arm. Zucchini, brussel sprouts, celery, spinach? Yuck, gross, ptooey. I could push lettuce around my plate indefinitely.

Now I am a Grownup, and I like vegetables more and more. Especially now that I make a point of eating fresh produce. I've learned to like vegetables for themselves, by themselves...steamed, tender, and lightly seasoned to release their inherent goodness. I've learned to appreciate produce in season, to find ingenious uses for zucchini when they overrun us every August. But I also relish that exquisite thrill of the first imported strawberry or asparagus, arriving here just when winter is about to drag off my soul in its icy clutches.

The following recipes suggest many ways to enjoy vegetables: some simply, by themselves with a pinch of seasoning, or partnered with other vegetables and dressed up in a sauce. One of the great pleasures of vegetarian dining is sitting down to a medley of fresh vegetables in season. It's almost a form of meditation to reclaim that simple pleasure: to savour the colour and crunch of vegetables, briefly sautéed or lightly steamed or just as is. Try a squeeze of lemon juice, a hint of garlic, and a cooked grain on the side with a splash of tamari. On particularly stressful days, a meal like this is exactly what I need to bring my mood up and my frazzle-level down. Nothing out of a box, nothing instant, no added colours or preservatives. Just good taste from food that's good for you. Pretty impressive, from someone who used to hate vegetables worse than homework.

BALSAMIC TOMATOES

2 or 3 large ripe tomatoes
2 T. minced fresh basil
1 or 2 T. balsamic or wine vinegar
salt, pepper to taste

Cut tomatoes in wedges or slices. Gently toss with basil, salt, and vinegar. Dust generously with freshly ground black pepper. Let rest for 20 minutes. Serve at room temperature.

TOMATOES PARMESAN

2 to 3 large tomatoes
4 T. Parmesan cheese
salt, pepper to taste
sprinkle of oregano
or paprika

PREHEAT BROILER UNIT OF OVEN. Trim the stems of the tomatoes, and any blemishes. Slice each tomato into 4 thick slices. Place on an oiled cookie sheet with a rim. Sprinkle each slice with Parmesan and seasonings. Broil for 5 to 10 minutes until tomatoes are browned. Serve immediately.

SPICY BREADED TOMATOES

3 large tomatoes
1 large egg, beaten with
2 T. milk, and a
dash of Worchestershire

1½ cups seasoned bread or cracker
    crumbs mixed with
salt, pepper to taste
dash of cayenne pepper
dash of dried mustard

4 T. olive or sunflower oil

Trim tomatoes and cut each one into 4 thick slices. Prepare the beaten egg in a bowl, and the bread crumbs on a plate. Dip each slice of tomato into the beaten egg, and then into the crumbs to coat both sides. Chill on waxed paper in fridge for 30 minutes to set. Heat oil in a cast-iron skillet. Brown tomatoes well on both sides. Serve piping hot.

SESAME CUCUMBERS

1 long English cucumber
2 T. toasted sesame oil
1 T. rice vinegar
2 T. gomasio (or toasted sesame seeds)
salt, pepper to taste

Score the cucumber with a fork to make vertical stripes in the green peel. Slice in ¼" thick slices. Toss all ingredients together in a decorative bowl. Chill for 20 to 30 minutes to allow flavours to develop.

LEMON ANISE CUCUMBERS

1 long English cucumber, cubed
¼ cup lemon juice
2 T. sunflower oil
1 T. lemon peel
1 t. anise seeds, lightly ground
salt, pepper to taste

Lightly grind the anise seeds by cracking them in a mortar and pestle or with a heavy can or jar. Mix juice, oil, and seasonings, and set aside for at least 30 minutes to develop flavours. Toss cucumbers with the dressing; serve.

MINTY CUCUMBERS

1 long English cucumber, halved
   lengthwise and thinly sliced
¾ cup yogurt
1 t. honey
⅓ cup fresh mint, minced
¼ cup fresh parsley, minced
pepper to taste

Thoroughly mix the yogurt and honey. Toss with cucumber and herbs. Chill; stir just before serving. Sprinkle with freshly ground pepper.

DIJON CUCUMBERS

¼ cup sunflower oil
1 clove garlic, minced
1 T. dijon mustard
1 T. lemon juice
¼ cup fresh parsley, minced
salt, pepper to taste

Mix dressing ingredients together thoroughly with a fork.

1 long English cucumber, julienned
1 red bell pepper, julienned

Toss the julienned vegetables with the dressing. Chill for 15 to 20 minutes for the flavours to develop.

TRI-COLOUR PEPPER TRIANGLES

1 to 2 T. sweet white miso
3 T. sake or mirin
dash of cayenne pepper

Blend together until smooth. Set aside.

1 large green bell pepper
1 large red bell pepper
1 large yellow bell pepper
1 to 2 T. sesame oil

Prepare the peppers by trimming ends, seeds, and membranes. Cut into strips 1" wide, then slice on the diagonal to form triangles. Heat oil in a wok until very hot, but not smoking. Stirfry peppers for 2 to 3 minutes. Remove from heat, toss with miso dressing. Serve steaming.

PEPPER AND ZUCCHINI SAUTÉ

1 medium red onion
1 medium green bell pepper
1 medium red bell pepper
1 medium yellow bell pepper
2 medium zucchini
1 large tomato

Cut the red onion into crescents. Remove seeds, tips, and membranes from the peppers, and slice into strips. Slice the zucchini into ½" rounds. Chop the tomato coarsely.

2 T. olive oil
4 cloves garlic, minced
1 T. rosemary
2 t. oregano
salt, pepper to taste
¼ cup lemon juice

Heat the oil in a large skillet. Add prepared vegetables, garlic and herbs. Sauté for several minutes over medium high heat, stirring constantly, until vegetables are lightly browned. Add lemon juice. Season to taste, and serve immediately.

ROASTED RED PEPPERS IN OIL

4 large unblemished red bell peppers
2 T. good quality olive oil
salt, pepper to taste
2 cloves garlic, minced (optional)
1 sprig fresh sage or basil (optional)

PREHEAT OVEN TO 450° F. Trim tips, seeds, and membranes from peppers. Place on a rimmed baking sheet and bake for 15 to 20 minutes until blackened and blistered all over. (Alternate method: pierce with a long fork and hold over gas element on stove.) Set aside, covered with a cloth, until cool enough to handle. Peel away all the burnt skin and slice peppers in half. Place in a bowl with oil and seasonings. Let rest for 20 minutes. Drain; serve spread on crusty rolls, or with pasta.

CIDER CARROTS

3 large carrots, peeled and sliced on
    the diagonal
1 cup apple cider
½ t. nutmeg
¼ t. ground clove
1 T. honey
2 T. lemon juice
1 T. butter
salt, pepper to taste

Place all ingredients in a heavy-bottomed pot. Bring to the boil; reduce heat; cover and simmer for 10 to 12 minutes. Uncover and simmer a few more minutes until carrots are just tender. Serve warm.

LEMON-BRAISED CARROTS

3 T. oil
1 small onion, minced
3 cups julienned
carrots

Heat oil in a skillet over medium high heat. Sauté onion and carrots, stirring constantly, until lightly browned.

⅓ cup water
⅓ cup lemon juice
zest of one lemon
3 T. fresh dill (or 1 T. dried)
salt, pepper to taste

Add liquids, zest, and seasonings, and bring to the boil. Reduce heat; stir; cover. Simmer for 5 to 7 minutes, or until carrots are tender.

BUTTERMILK MASHED POTATOES

4 cups water
1 t. salt
3 large potatoes, peeled

Bring salted water to the boil. Add potatoes; cook, uncovered for 15 to 20 minutes until potatoes are tender.

¼ to ⅓ cup buttermilk or milk
1 T. oil or butter
¼ cup fresh parsley, minced
salt, pepper to taste

Drain potatoes thoroughly. Return to the pot; add buttermilk and oil. With a potato masher or electric beater, mash until smooth. Stir in parsley, adjust seasoning. Serve piping hot.

MASHED SWEET POTATOES WITH PECANS

4 cups water
½ t. salt
3 large sweet potatoes, peeled and cubed

Bring salted water to the boil. Add potatoes, cook uncovered for 15 minutes, or until potatoes are tender.

¼ to ⅓ cup orange juice
1 T. butter or margarine
1 to 2 T. honey or molasses
salt, pepper to taste
sprinkle of nutmeg
½ cup toasted, chopped pecans

Drain sweet potatoes thoroughly. Return to the pot. Add juice, honey, seasonings, and butter. With a potato masher or electric beater, mash until smooth. Stir in pecans. Taste; adjust seasoning. Serve immediately. Minced fresh parsley makes an attractive garnish.

INDONESIAN GREEN BEANS WITH GINGER AND CHILIS

This fresh and fiery dish will win your heart. Carrots or sweet peppers make an appetizing variation.

SERVES 4

1 lb. (approx. 3 cups) fresh green beans

Trim ends from beans and cut them into 2" lengths. Set aside.

4 T. sunflower oil
1 small fresh hot chili, seeded and minced
4 large cloves garlic, minced
1" fresh ginger, peeled and grated
1 bay leaf
1 small onion, cut into crescents

Place a wok over high heat. When hot, carefully add the oil. When the oil is hot, add chili and seasonings. Stirfry for one minute. Add onion and green beans and stirfry for an additional 3 minutes.

½ cup water
1½ cups bean sprouts
salt to taste

Add water and salt to green beans. Cover, reduce heat. Simmer for 5 minutes. Stir in the bean sprouts during the last minute of cooking. Serve over rice, with Baked Marinated Tofu, p. 27.

GREEN BEANS IN
CAJUN PECAN SAUCE

*The Cajun bite of Louisiana cookin' makes this sauce
magic over sautéed spinach as well as carrots.*

SERVES 4

4 T. oil
1 large red onion, cut into crescents
3 cloves garlic, minced
1 lb. fresh green beans, trimmed and
    cut in half
1 T. lemon zest
4 T. lemon juice
6 T. beer or vegetable stock
dash of Worchestershire
dash of Tabasco
1 t. dried ground thyme
salt, pepper to taste

Heat oil in a large skillet. Sauté onion, garlic, and green beans until onions are browned. Add lemon zest and juice, beer, and seasonings. Simmer, covered, for 10 minutes, or until green beans are just tender. Taste; adjust seasonings.

1 cup toasted pecan pieces

Toss the beans with toasted pecans. Serve immediately.

TO TOAST PECANS

PREHEAT OVEN TO 400° F. Place pecans on a rimmed baking sheet. Toast for 7 to 10 minutes, stirring often. Watch carefully: nuts burn quickly! When evenly browned, remove from oven; let cool. Chop the nuts, if desired. Toast extra nuts and store in the freezer for future use.

BRAISED BUTTERNUT SQUASH

A plainly delicious Oriental treatment of winter squash.

SERVES 4

2 lb. squash
(butternut, acorn or other hard winter
    squash or pumpkin)
2 T. canola or peanut oil
4 to 5 cloves garlic, minced

Cut the squash in half and scoop out all the seeds and fibres. Then cut the squash into wedges or strips for easier handling. Pare away the outside rind, and cut the squash into 1" cubes.

Heat the oil over medium heat in a wok with a lid. Carefully add the squash cubes, stirring gently to coat with oil. Fry for 2 minutes.

⅓ cup water or vegetable stock
2 T. sake or mirin
1 T. salt (optional)

Carefully pour liquids into the wok; turn up the heat and bring to a rapid boil. Cover. Reduce heat to low and simmer for 10 to 15 minutes, until the squash is tender and the liquid has almost evaporated.

freshly ground black pepper

Dust the cooked squash with pepper and serve immediately.

INDONESIAN COCONUT SAUCE
FOR CARROTS AND CAULIFLOWER

An exotic and delicious way to eat everyday vegetables.

SERVES 4

⅓ cup dried grated coconut
¼ cup hot water

Combine coconut and water in a small bowl and set aside for 30 minutes.

½ medium red bell pepper, seeded and chopped
4 cloves garlic
4 T. lime juice
1 t. honey
1 t. chili powder
salt to taste

Process red pepper and seasonings together in a blender or food processor until smooth. Pour in the rehydrated coconut for a final brief burst. Set aside.

8 cups water
1 T. salt
1 medium head cauliflower, broken into small florets
3 medium carrots, peeled and julienned

Bring water to a rolling boil in a large pot. Add salt, cauliflower, and carrots. Boil for 5 to 7 minutes until vegetables are tender, but still crisp. Drain quickly. Toss with coconut sauce in a large serving bowl while still warm. May be served warm or chilled.

For a delicious Indonesian meal, serve these vegetables and Indonesian Green Beans with Ginger and Chilis (p. 99), beside a platter of steaming rice. For an authentic Indonesian presentation, decorate the platter with fresh parsley or cilantro, slices of hard-boiled egg, and chopped peanuts.

DEVILLED CAULIFLOWER

This simple, tangy dijon creme is also excellent over broccoli.

1 head cauliflower	Break the cauliflower into florets. Steam for 10 to 15 minutes, until barely tender.
4 T. dijon mustard ⅓ cup lowfat yogurt ⅓ cup mayonnaise 2 to 3 T. milk salt, pepper to taste	Mix dressing with a fork until thoroughly blended. Toss gently with the steamed cauliflower.
paprika	Sprinkle paprika generously over the cauliflower, and toss to spread the colour. Serve warm.

This dressing is also lovely with a chilled vegetable salad. Prepare the dressing; toss with lightly steamed vegetables (½ head cauliflower and ½ head broccoli broken into florets, 1 cup diced carrots, and 1 cup peas or snow peas.) Refrigerate for 2 hours; serve at room temperature. Very good to take to work if you have a fridge to keep it in.

ANTIPASTO

*Crisp vegetables marinated in olive oil and balsamic
vinegar make a perfect accompaniment to pasta or pizza.
Superb as a summer supper nestled in a bed of lettuce,
with olives, cheese wedges, and a crusty bread.*

SERVES 4 TO 6

2 cups cauliflower, broken into large
    florets
2 cups broccoli, broken into large
    florets
1 large carrot, peeled and sliced on the
    diagonal

Steam vegetables over boiling
water for 10 to 15 minutes until
tender, but still crisp. Drain.

½ cup good quality olive oil
1 clove garlic, crushed
¼ cup balsamic or wine vinegar
1 or 2 sprigs fresh dill or basil or
    mint
salt, pepper to taste
sprinkle of crushed dried chilis
    (optional)

½ English cucumber, sliced
1 cup mushrooms, rinsed and cut in
    half

While vegetables are steaming,
combine oil, vinegar, and
seasonings. Mix thoroughly.
Pour the dressing over the hot,
drained vegetables. Toss gently
until coated. When the
vegetables have cooled slightly,
add cucumber slices and
mushrooms. Toss again. Chill in
fridge for 1 hour. Drain; serve at
room temperature.

Antipasto is best made one day ahead, to allow flavours to
soak into the vegetables. It keeps well for 2 or 3 days in the
fridge. Substitute or add cherry tomatoes, steamed green
beans, steamed fennel bulb slices, roasted red pepper slices,
leek slices, steamed tiny pearl onions, or celery sticks.

BRUSSEL SPROUTS WITH WALNUT DRESSING

I've included a recipe for those of you who, for your own inexplicable reasons actually like brussel sprouts. (Someone must like them, because farmers keep growing them.) This recipe was contributed by my friend John Ghitan, who is a fabulous cook. Brussel sprouts make a nice accompaniment to holiday dinners.

SERVES 4

1 lb. brussel sprouts

Trim and discard the outer leaves and the stalk. Steam the brussel sprouts, covered, for 10 to 15 minutes until barely tender. Plunge into cold water to cool; drain thoroughly.

¼ cup lemon juice
3 T. balsamic vinegar
3 T. dijon mustard
1 T. honey
salt, pepper to taste
⅓ cup fresh parsley

Blend briefly in a blender or food processor.

⅔ cup canola oil

With motor running, trickle oil in a slow steady stream into the blender. Blend until thoroughly mixed.

½ cup walnut pieces, toasted

Combine steamed brussel sprouts in a bowl with walnuts and dressing; toss until coated. Serve at room temperature.

SANTA FE BEANS

Chilis and seasonings light a Southwestern spark in plain beans. Eat these refried beans tucked into a taco, on nachos, with cheese melted on top, or as a dip for chips, with Salsa Picante, p. 208.

p. 208

SERVES 4 TO 6

3 cups cooked pinto beans, drained
    (reserving liquid)
¼ to ⅓ cup reserved liquid from
    beans
salt to taste

Mash the cooked, drained beans thoroughly with a potato masher, adding small amounts of the reserved liquid to obtain the desired consistency. (Refried beans should be thick, but spreadable.) Set aside.

2 T. sunflower oil
2 or 3 cloves garlic, minced
1 medium onion, diced
1 small red bell pepper, diced
1 small yellow bell pepper, diced
1 (4 oz.) can roasted green chilis,
    diced
⅓ cup fresh basil, minced
¼ cup fresh parsley or cilantro,
    minced
2 t. cumin
salt, pepper, picante sauce to taste

Heat oil in a cast-iron skillet. Sauté onion and garlic for 6 to 7 minutes. Add peppers and seasonings; sauté 3 to 4 more minutes until peppers are tender.

Add the mashed beans to the skillet. Keep cooking and stirring until the beans and peppers are thoroughly mixed and heated throughout. Serve hot as a side dish or taco filling, or at room temperature as a dip for corn chips.

THE MAIN COURSE

And now for the main course!

For your dining pleasure tonight we offer Japanese noodles with stirfried broccoli, in a spicy almond sauce.

Or does the steamy intrigue of Cajun Okra Gumbo match your mood?

Perhaps I can tempt you with a fragrant pilaf of tender couscous and apricots?

Tonight's special is a sizzling platter of tempeh strips broiled in lime juice, wrapped in warmed flour tortillas with grilled peppers and sour cream.

Maybe you just need some good home-cooking.
We got spaghetti like mamma used to make it.
C'mon, what'll it be?
You want I should make you a sandwich?

RATATOUILLE

A traditional vegetable medley from the south of France.
Serve over couscous, rice, or pasta, with a simple green salad.

SERVES 4

1 small eggplant, peeled and cut into 1" cubes

Soak eggplant cubes in very salty water for 30 minutes. Drain; rinse well and drain again. Set aside.

¼ cup olive oil
1 onion, chopped
3 cloves garlic, minced
2 cups cauliflower florets
3 cups chopped fresh tomatoes [or 1 (28 oz.) can]
1 bay leaf
1 T. dried oregano
½ t. dried thyme
salt, pepper to taste
1 small fresh fennel bulb, trimmed and finely diced
½ cup red wine (or 2 T. wine vinegar and ⅓ c. water)
1 cup mushrooms, halved
2 cups chopped zucchini
¼ cup fresh parsley, minced

Heat oil in a large heavy-bottomed skillet. Sauté onions, garlic, and cauliflower for 5 minutes over medium high heat. Reduce heat to medium. Add tomatoes, fennel, drained eggplant, and seasonings; simmer for an additional 15 minutes, stirring occasionally. Add wine, mushrooms, and zucchini; stir; simmer for a final 10 minutes. For the final minute of cooking, stir in fresh parsley. Serve steaming hot over cooked rice, couscous, or pasta.

Variations: Omit the fennel and substitute other fresh herbs (thyme, tarragon, dill). Substitute or add fresh green beans, green or red peppers, artichoke hearts, yellow squash, or carrots for any of the vegetables listed. Also pleasant as a side dish, served at room temperature.

TEMPEH FAJITAS

Strips of broiled tempeh marinated in lime, wrapped in a flour tortilla with peppers, onions, salsa, and cheese...a delicious vegetarian version of a popular Tex-Mex dish. Invite a group of friends to assemble their own fajitas. Serve Santa Fe Beans (p. 106) on the side.

SERVES 4

2 (250 gram) pkgs. tempeh, thawed
3 T. oil
3 T. tamari
3 T. lime juice
1 T. chili powder
pepper to taste

Using a long serrated knife, cut each square of tempeh in half through the middle to form two thin sheets. Cut each sheet into 4 strips. In a measuring cup, combine oil, tamari, lime juice, and seasonings. Spoon half of this marinade over a rimmed baking sheet. Lay out the tempeh strips in the marinade, and spoon remaining liquid over the strips. Let rest for 30 minutes. **TURN ON THE BROILER UNIT OF THE OVEN.** Drain the tempeh, reserving the marinade. Place the strips under the broiler at a distance of 6 to 8" and broil for 7 minutes on each side.

2 T. oil
2 medium onions, cut into crescents
1 small green bell pepper, julienned
1 small red bell pepper, julienned

Heat oil in a skillet. Sauté onions and peppers until well browned. Pour leftover marinade over the vegetables. Heat throughout; keep warm.

CONTINUED

8 to 12 *flour tortillas*
2 *medium tomatoes, diced*
1 *cup sour cream or yogurt*
1 ½ *cups cheddar cheese, grated*
1 *to* 2 *cups picante sauce*
2 *limes, cut into wedges*

Heat the tortillas on a griddle or in the oven; wrap them in a towel or foil to keep warm. Arrange tempeh and sautéed peppers on a platter. Place tomatoes and other toppings in small decorative bowls within easy reach. Invite each guest to load a warmed tortilla with tempeh, peppers, the condiments of her choice, and a squeeze of lime juice. For a real feast, serve with refried beans, guacamole (p. 153), and corn tortilla chips.

For authentic flavour, cook the marinated tempeh on a barbeque grill. The flour tortillas may also be heated over the flames: lay them briefly on the grill, turning once. And while you're grilling outside, why not husk several ears of corn, butter them, and cook them on the barbeque?

ZESTY SESAME –
VEGETABLE MEDLEY

*A tangy selection of sautéed vegetables. Serve on a bed
of pasta or fluffy grain for a satisfying dinner.*

SERVES 4

¼ cup sesame oil
⅓ cup sesame seeds
1 cup onion crescents
1½ cups julienned carrots
1½ cups trimmed green beans
2 cups chopped tomatoes
5 cloves garlic, minced

Heat oil in heavy skillet. Add sesame seeds and vegetables; sauté for 5 minutes.

1 cup julienned zucchini
splash of Worcestershire sauce
¼ cup picante sauce
3 T. tamari
black pepper to taste
1 cup vegetable stock or tomato juice

Add zucchini and seasonings. Sauté for an additional 5 minutes. Pour in the juice or stock and simmer for 10 minutes.

2 cups chopped fresh spinach leaves,
    trimmed and well-rinsed
sprinkle of grated nutmeg
1 cup lowfat yogurt (mixed with
    2 T. flour)

Add spinach, nutmeg, and yogurt. Simmer for a final 5 minutes. Taste; adjust seasoning. Serve hot over bulghar wheat, rice, or pasta.

FRIJOLE CORN PIE

A classic example of complementary proteins, this tasty and filling savoury pie hails from the American Southwest.

SERVES 6

3 cups water
1⅓ cups cornmeal
1 t. salt
1 T. chili powder
2 T. oil or butter
2 T. dried parsley (or
6 T. fresh, minced)

Bring water to the boil in a heavy-bottomed pan (preferably nonstick). Stir in the corn meal, oil, and seasonings. Simmer, stirring occasionally, for 20 to 25 minutes. The cornmeal should be thick, rather than runny. Spoon the thickened cornmeal into a lightly oiled 10" deep dish pie plate. Use the back of a spoon to spread the cornmeal evenly over the bottom and sides of the pan. The crust should be about 1" thick.

4 T. oil
1 medium onion, diced
1 medium green pepper, diced
1 red pepper, diced
4 cloves garlic, minced
1 (4 oz.) can diced roasted green chilis
dash of Worchestershire
salt, pepper to taste
2 T. ground cumin

Heat oil in a skillet. Brown the onion and the peppers with seasonings.
PREHEAT OVEN TO 350° F.

3 cups cooked pinto or kidney beans, drained
½ cup sour cream
3 to 5 T. picante sauce (to taste)

Combine beans, sour cream, and picante sauce with the browned onions. Mix well; heat over medium high heat for 10 to 15 minutes, stirring gently. Fill the cornmeal crust with the bean mixture; level with a knife or spatula.

CONTINUED

1 ½ cups grated cheese (cheddar or
     Monterey Jack)
dash of chili powder
1 green onion, diced

Sprinkle cheese evenly over the pie. Top with a dusting of chili powder and diced green onion for colour. Bake for 20 minutes, until the pie is heated throughout and the cheese has melted.

METRIC/IMPERIAL CONVERSIONS

1 teaspoon (t.) = 5 millilitres (ml)
1 tablespoon (T.) = 15 millilitres (ml)
1 cup = approximately 250 ml
1 ounce (oz.) = approximately 30 grams
2.2 pounds (lbs.) = 1 kilogram
1 inch (") = 2.54 centimetres (cm)

VEGETABLE GOULASH

*This hearty winter stew draws flavour and sturdiness
from its Eastern European roots. Serve with a
crusty bread and pickled beets.*

SERVES 4

2 large potatoes, cubed
2 medium carrots, sliced
2 cups celeriac or turnip or parsnip,
   peeled and cubed
1 bay leaf
water or vegetable stock
1 t. salt

Place vegetables in a large soup
pot. Add just enough water or
vegetable stock to cover. Bring
to the boil. Reduce heat, cover,
and simmer for 20 minutes.

1 (28 oz.) can tomatoes

Chop tomatoes coarsely. Add
with tomato juice to the soup
pot. Simmer, stirring occasionally.

3 T. oil
1 medium onion, chopped
1 T. Hungarian paprika
2 T. dried marjoram
1 T. tarragon or parsley
2 T. caraway seeds
1 t. black pepper
2 cups chopped green cabbage
2 cups sliced mushrooms
½ to 1 cup water, as needed

Heat oil in a large skillet. Sauté
onions until translucent. Add
seasonings, cabbage, and
mushrooms. Continue to sauté
for 10 minutes, stirring often.
(Note: paprika scorches easily,
so be prepared to reduce the
heat.)
Add to the stew; stir to
combine. Adjust seasonings;
pour in water as needed to
obtain desired consistency;
simmer for 10 more minutes.
Serve hot.

SESAME FRIED RICE

*Fried rice is a perennial favourite at Chinese restaurants.
Tofu cubes and sesame seeds are the stars of this version.
A one-pan dish that's a meal in itself, and quickly
concocted if you have cooked rice on hand.*

SERVES 4

3 cups cooked rice

(If you need rice, cook one cup rice in 3 cups water.) Set cooked rice aside.

1 block firm tofu, pressed & drained
3 T. tamari
2 T. oil

Cut tofu into small cubes about ½" square. Place cubed tofu in a small bowl; sprinkle with tamari. Let rest for several minutes. Heat oil in a large skillet or wok; when it is very hot, carefully add the tofu. Brown the tofu by flipping gently with a wooden spatula or spoon. When browned on all sides, remove from skillet and set aside.

2 T. toasted sesame oil
2 T. oil
1 clove star anise
1 hot dried chili
1 medium onion, finely diced
2 medium carrots, finely diced
2 stalks celery, finely diced
3 cloves garlic, minced
1" fresh ginger, grated
¼ cup sesame seeds
½ t. nutmeg

Heat oil in the skillet used for tofu. Drop in star anise and chili. Stirfry vegetables and seasonings quickly over high heat for 4 to 5 minutes, stirring often. Remove and discard star anise and chili.

CONTINUED

2 T. oil
½ cup frozen peas
1 cup diced Napa cabbage or
cabbage
4 T. tamari
black pepper to taste

Add the cooked rice and remaining ingredients to skillet; stir well to combine rice evenly with vegetables. Fry 3 to 5 minutes over medium high heat, stirring constantly, until heated throughout. Gently mix in the tofu cubes. Serve hot.

Substitute or add green onions, snow peas, Chinese baby corn, water chestnuts, or broccoli florets for any of the vegetables listed. Substitute cooked tempeh cubes or cooked aduki beans or nuts for the cooked tofu. Serve snow peas or broccoli stirfried with garlic on the side.

SLOPPY SAMS

A vegetarian version of a childhood classic.

SERVES 4

1 cup brown or red lentils, well-rinsed
3 cups water

Bring water to the boil. (Add ½ t. salt if desired.) Add lentils; boil over medium heat for 30 minutes or until tender, stirring occasionally.

4 T. olive oil
1 cup chopped onions

2 cups chopped tomatoes
2 cloves garlic, minced

3 oz. tomato paste
½ cup ketchup
1 t. dried mustard
2 t. chili powder
2 to 3 T. molasses
dash of Worchestershire
salt, pepper to taste

While lentils are cooking, heat oil in a skillet. Sauté onions until translucent over medium high heat. Add tomatoes and garlic; sauté for 5 minutes. Add tomato paste, ketchup, and seasonings, simmer the stew for 5 to 10 minutes. When lentils are tender, add to tomato sauce (adding or draining cooking liquid as needed to obtain the desired consistency). Stir and heat thoroughly. Serve hot over open-faced buns or rice.

STEW À LA TARRAGON

*A character-building stew of vegetables and beans, highlighted by tarragon
and mustard. The vegetables are cooked covered, in very little liquid, so that
they are partly simmered and partly steamed...they absorb the flavour of
the seasonings very well this way. Quick to make if you use canned beans,
and a good autumn supper served with cornbread.*

SERVES 4

4 T. olive oil
2 cups chopped carrots
2 cups chopped onions
6 cloves garlic, minced
2 T. dried tarragon
1 t. dried mustard
salt, pepper to taste

Heat oil in a heavy pot with a
lid. Sauté the carrots, covered,
for 5 minutes over medium high
heat, stirring occasionally. Add
onion, garlic, and seasonings.
Sauté for another 5 minutes.

1 cup chopped red pepper
3 green onions, diced
3 tomatoes, chopped
1 cup corn kernels
2 packed cups chopped greens
 (spinach or kale or collard),
 well-rinsed
½ cup vegetable stock or liquid from
 beans

Reduce heat to medium. Add
peppers and green onions,
cover; sauté 5 more minutes.
Add tomatoes, greens, corn, and
liquid. Stir to combine and
cover; simmer until all
vegetables are tender.

3 cups cooked kidney beans with
 some liquid

Add the beans to the cooked
vegetables. Stir, cover; simmer
until just heated throughout.
Taste; adjust seasoning. Serve
hot, over cornbread, rice, or
bulghar.

Substitute any other kind of cooked bean. Try celery or
turnip or potato instead of the vegetables listed. If desired,
sprinkle grated cheese over each serving. This recipe also
works well as a vegetable side dish; omit the beans to serve
with quiche or Pasta Carbonara.

OKRA GUMBO

Originally native to Africa, okra has been embraced by the American South. In the Cajun country of Louisiana, it picked up the French accent you'll enjoy in this thick spicy stew with a tomato base. Foraging for a living in their swampy homeland, Cajuns would traditionally have used vegetables in their gumbo plus whatever they could catch...chicken, duck, shrimp, crawfish, fish, pork or sausage, even alligator. (We'll skip the 'gator for our gumbo.) Under Cajun influence, okra gumbo has become a byword for joie d'vivre...eat it over rice, with some cornbread on the side.

SERVES 4

1 T. oil
3 T. flour
salt, pepper to taste

In the bottom of a large soup pot, stir together flour and oil with a whisk or a fork. Cook over low heat for 15 to 20 minutes, stirring occasionally, until the roux is a rich brown. DO NOT BURN. Remove the roux to a bowl; set aside.

3 T. oil
1 pound okra, rinsed, trimmed, and cut into ¼" slices
2 medium onions, chopped
6 cloves garlic, minced
2 stalks celery, chopped

In the same pot, heat oil and sauté the okra, onions, garlic, and celery over medium high heat until well-browned. Reduce heat; add peppers, seasonings, and the tomatoes. Simmer for 15 minutes.

1 red bell pepper, chopped
1 green bell pepper, chopped
1 (28 oz.) can tomatoes, drained, coarsely chopped, and juice reserved
dash of Tabasco
dash of Worchestershire
2 bay leaves
1 t. thyme
salt to taste
lots of black pepper

CONTINUED

2 cups boiling water or vegetable
   stock

Whisk together water, reserved juice from tomatoes, and the roux, until smooth. Mix thoroughly with the vegetables. Cover. Over low heat, simmer the stew for 30 minutes, adding additional water if needed. Taste and adjust seasonings (should be bold, flavourful, and peppery). Serve hot over rice, and pass extra Tabasco for those souls brave enough to like their gumbo extra hot.

TO MAKE A ROUX:

A roux is a mixture of flour and oil or butter browned together and used to thicken sauces. The secret to a succesful roux is to slowly cook the flour and oil in a heavy skillet, so that it very gradually browns without burning; the darker brown the roux, the richer the flavour. Once the roux is cooked, it can be whisked into stock, sauces or stews as a thickener. Rouxs cooked with oil can be stored for several weeks in a sealed container in the refrigerator, to be used a spoonful at a time as needed.

MUSHROOM TOFU SUKIYAKI

The vegetarian version of a Japanese standard. Once the ingredients are prepared, this dish comes together very quickly. An electric skillet, if you have one, works best, and you can cook the sukiyaki right at the table. A large skillet or wok also works well. Serve over rice, with shredded lettuce and fresh tomato wedges on the side.

SERVES 4

1 block tofu, pressed and drained
tamari

PREHEAT OVEN TO 400° F.
Slice tofu into ¼" slices. Dip each slice in tamari, turning to coat both sides. Bake on an oiled baking sheet for 15 minutes until well-browned. Remove from oven. When cool enough to handle, cut each slice crosswise into thin strips. Set aside.

¼ cup oil
1 large onion, cut into crescents
2 T. minced fresh ginger
1 large carrot, peeled and grated
4 stalks celery with leaves, sliced
    thinly on the diagonal
black pepper to taste

While tofu is baking, prepare the vegetables and pile them in their separate groups on a platter. (Some vegetables take longer to cook than others.) When tofu is cooked and vegetables are cut, heat oil in skillet over high heat. Stirfry onion and ginger for 2 to 3 minutes. Reduce heat slightly, add carrots and celery; cook for another 2 minutes.

CONTINUED

1 lb. mushrooms, rinsed and thinly
   sliced
2 cups Napa cabbage (or green
   cabbage or spinach), shredded
3 to 6 T. tamari
3 to 6 T. vegetable stock or water
2 cups mung bean sprouts, rinsed and
   drained

Add mushrooms, cabbage and
sliced tofu to skillet. Splash in a
little tamari and stock
occasionally – just enough to
evaporate fairly quickly,
sending up a fragrant steam but
not flooding the vegetables.
Sauté for 3 to 4 minutes. Add
sprouts and sauté for a final 2
minutes. Serve immediately
over rice.

ALOO GOBI
(POTATO AND CAULIFLOWER CURRY)

*This classic curry is one of my favourite Indian dishes.
The mild base of potatoes and cauliflower allows all the
flavours of the curry to come through separately,
as well as in harmony.*

SERVES 4

6 T. sunflower oil
1 medium onion, diced
1" fresh ginger, grated
2 T. cumin seeds
3 T. mustard seeds
2 t. turmeric
2 t. salt
1 dried hot chili, seeded and crumbled
    (or splash of hot chili oil)

Heat oil in a large wok or skillet with a closely-fitting lid. When oil is hot, add onion and seasonings. Sauté until onion is soft.

6 medium potatoes, scrubbed and
    diced
(about 4 cups)
¼ to ½ cup water

Add diced raw potatoes to the onions, and stirfry over high heat for 3 to 5 minutes, stirring constantly. Reduce heat to medium; add ¼ cup water to the wok. Cover tightly: the trapped steam will help cook the potatoes. Stir occasionally. Keep an eye on the water, and as it evaporates, keep adding very small quantities to the wok.

1 medium head cauliflower

While the potatoes are cooking, cut the cauliflower into bite-sized florets (the same size as the potato pieces). When the potatoes are about halfway tender, add the florets to the wok. Stir gently so that the vegetables do not disintegrate. Replace the lid and continue to cook until the vegetables are tender. Stir gently every once in a while.

½ cup minced leaves of fresh mint or cilantro, trimmed and rinsed
½ cup finely diced red pepper or frozen peas

Add to potatoes for the last 2 minutes of cooking. Taste and adjust seasonings, especially salt. Stir thoroughly, but gently. Serve hot, with rice, chick peas, or Indian bread.

LORRAINE'S QUICHE

I stole this recipe from my friends Lorraine and George Newman. They first served me this easy quiche, with its crust made from bread, on the deck of their cottage in the Muskokas. (A tough life, but someone has to live it.)

SERVES 6 TO 8

3 to 4 slices of toasted bread

PREHEAT OVEN TO 350° F. Cut toast into strips; use to line the bottom of an oiled 9 x 13" casserole pan.

2 T. oil
1 medium onion, diced
2 cloves garlic, minced
2 t. blend of dried marjoram, oregano, basil, dill, or tarragon
salt, pepper to taste
1 ½ cups sliced mushrooms or broccoli florets or zucchini

Heat oil in a skillet. Add onion, garlic, and herbs. Sauté over medium high heat for 7 minutes. Add the vegetable(s) and sauté for 3 more minutes. Spread evenly over the toast-lined casserole.

8 to 10 eggs, beaten
1 ¾ cups milk
pinch of salt and pepper
dash of nutmeg

Mix together eggs, milk, and seasonings. Pour gently over the vegetable layer.

2 cups grated Swiss or cheddar cheese

Sprinkle cheese evenly over the casserole. Bake for 35 minutes, or until a knife inserted in the centre comes out clean. Serve warm. (Leftovers make a tasty cold lunch the next day.)

CONTINUED

This remarkable quiche is quickly prepared, and flexibly accepts substitutions. Rye, whole wheat, or multigrain bread makes an interesting crust. Substitute chopped spinach or corn kernels or tomato slices for the vegetables listed. Vary the seasoning to complement the rest of your menu. Fresh herbs are particularly nice.

SPICY BROCCOLI NOODLES

Japanese noodles with broccoli in a spicy almond-garlic sauce. Cucumber slices and a light miso soup make the ideal dinner companions.

SERVES 4

6 oz. udon or soba noodles

Bring a large pot of salted water to the boil. Drop in the noodles. Boil 10 to 12 minutes until tender, stirring occasionally. Drain noodles and set aside.

2 T. oil
4 cloves garlic, minced
1 small hot dried chili
¼ cup vinegar (rice or apple cider)
⅓ cup tamari
1 T. honey
½ cup almond butter

In a saucepan, heat oil and sauté the garlic with chili until browned. Reduce heat; add vinegar, tamari, honey, and almond butter. Stir well until thoroughly blended. Simmer for 5 minutes, but do not boil, and be careful to avoid scorching. Keep sauce warm until ready to use.

2 T. oil
1 cup onion crescents
1 red bell pepper, julienned
2 cups broccoli, sliced (stems and flowers)

Heat oil in a large wok. Stirfry onions, and broccoli for 3 minutes; add red pepper and stirfry for another 3 minutes. Add noodles and sauce to the wok, tossing well to combine. Stirfry until heated throughout.

Toasted almond slivers

Sprinkle with almond slivers before serving. Delightful hot or cold.

SUMMER FRITTERS

Light vegetable cakes, seasoned with herbs and panfried.
Combine with Cider Carrots (p.97) and a grain pilaf
for an inviting summer supper.

SERVES 4

1 medium onion, minced
1 cup grated zucchini
2 cups corn kernels
2 t. salt
1 t. black pepper
1 T. dried tarragon or dill
2 T. milk
4 to 6 T. flour

Mix all ingredients except egg whites and oil together in a bowl. Chill in fridge for 20 minutes.

2 egg whites

In a clean, cool bowl, whip the egg whites until they form stiff peaks, using a whisk or an electric mixer. Fold gently into the vegetable batter until completely incorporated. Batter should hold together. If too wet, gently fold in 1 or 2 more tablespoons of flour.

4 T. oil

Heat oil in a skillet. Spoon the batter into the hot oil to form cakes about 3" wide. Cook over medium high heat until browned on one side. Gently turn the cakes over to brown the other side. Remove from heat, drain on a paper towel-lined plate. Keep finished cakes warm in a very low oven while cooking the rest of the batch.

CASHEW VEGETABLE STIRFRY

*Stirfried vegetables over rice are one of the foundations
of a vegetarian diet: a colourful, nourishing, and speedy
meal that utilizes the vegetables you have on hand.
Cashews add protein, texture, and richness.*

SERVES 4

2 T. sunflower oil
2 T. toasted sesame oil
4 cloves garlic, minced
1" fresh ginger, minced
1 small dried hot chili
1 medium onion, cut into cresents
1 large carrot, peeled and sliced on the
    diagonal
2 stalks celery, sliced on the diagonal

Heat oil in a large wok or skillet. When oil is very hot, but not smoking, add ginger, garlic, and chili. Stirfry for 30 seconds; add onion, carrot, and celery. Stirring frequently, cook over medium high heat for 3 to 5 minutes until vegetables are barely tender.

1 red or green bell pepper, julienned
1 bunch green onions, cut in 1"
    lengths
8 to 10 mushrooms, sliced
2 cups snow peas or shredded
    cabbage or bok choy
1 cup cashews, roasted or raw

Add peppers, green onions, mushrooms, cabbage, and cashews to the onions. Continue to stirfry for another 3 minutes.

1 cup bean sprouts
¼ cup tamari

Add sprouts and tamari; toss and stirfry for one more minute. Remove from heat and serve immediately over rice or bulghar wheat.

HOW TO STIRFRY

Stirfrying is a method of cooking over high heat, frying food in a small amount of oil very quickly while stirring almost constantly. Because the food cooks so rapidly, you need to have all the ingredients prepared before you begin. Cut the vegetables in attractive shapes, matchsticks or triangles or crescents – this makes the dish much more appealing. (Pretty food tastes better.) Quick cooking over high heat is the secret to success; the vegetables will retain their colour and most of their crispness.

Add or substitute almost any vegetable you have on hand: zucchini, peeled winter squash, eggplant, green beans, snow peas, shiitake mushrooms, spinach, kale, or canned Chinese specialties such as bamboo shoots, water chestnuts, or baby corn. Walnuts, almonds, cashews, or sesame seeds add protein (I prefer the flavour of roasted nuts, but raw nuts are acceptable). Cook cubes of tempeh or pressed, drained tofu before you add the vegetables: stirfry them separately, remove from the wok and reserve. Add them again at the end, tossing gently to prevent crumbling.

Some vegetables will cook more quickly than others. Arrange the prepared ingredients in separate bowls or in mounds on a tray near the stove, in the order that you will cook them. Onions, carrots, celery, and winter squash take the longest time to cook, so they go into the wok first. Peppers, sweet potatoes, mushrooms, zucchini, water chestnuts, nuts, and baby corn should be added next. Add leafy greens and bean sprouts at the last minute as they take very little cooking.

Garlic and ginger are the mainstays of an Oriental stirfry, but you can increase or decrease amounts to suit your personal taste. While stirfrying, add a pinch of nutmeg or a generous handful of fresh cilantro for flavour; or sprinkle on a combination of spices called Chinese Five Spice, or star anise, one of its component spices. You can omit the tamari at the end and toss the vegetables with sweet and sour sauce or hoisin, a rich, dark sauce found in Oriental shops. Or drain off any liquid from the vegetables into a small skillet, stir in 1 T. cornstarch dissolved in 2 T. water, ¼ cup orange juice, 1 t. honey and more tamari to taste. Heat until slightly thickened, stirring constantly, and pour back over vegetables. Serve hot.

A generous portion of stirfried vegetables over rice, bulghar wheat, couscous, or Japanese style noodles (udon or soba) can be a meal in itself. Serve stirfried vegetables as a side dish with marinated baked tofu. Pass extra tamari at the table for people to add, if desired. Chopsticks are especially appropriate when eating stirfried vegetables.

STUFFED ZUCCHINI

Stuffed with polenta, pine nuts, spinach, and cheese,
these "zukes" are filling as well as delicious.

SERVES 4

⅔ cup cornmeal
2 cups water
2 t. dried oregano
½ t. black pepper
1 t. salt
1 T. olive oil or butter

Bring water to the boil in a nonstick pot. Whisk in cornmeal and seasonings; return to the boil. Reduce heat and simmer 20 to 30 minutes, stirring occasionally until the polenta is thick and tender (See below for additions to the polenta in the final 5 minutes of cooking.) PREHEAT OVEN TO 375° F.

8 small zucchini, plump and
    evenly shaped

While the polenta is cooking, rinse the zucchini and split them in half lengthwise. Using a melon baller or a small knife, scoop out a trough from the centre of each squash to hold the filling. Be careful not to penetrate the skin of the zucchini. Place zucchini boats in a lightly oiled casserole. Carefully pour ¼ cup water around their bottoms. Bake for 20 minutes or until zucchini are tender. Remove from the oven, but leave the oven on.

CONTINUED

3 packed cups shredded, trimmed fresh
   spinach
½ cup pine nuts
½ cup Parmesan cheese
½ t. grated nutmeg
salt, pepper to taste

While zucchini are baking, rinse spinach thoroughly and drain. During the final 5 minutes of cooking the polenta, stir in spinach, pine nuts, cheese and seasonings. Cool until lukewarm to the touch.

Spoon the warm polenta into zucchini halves, mounding carefully. Sprinkle with a little Parmesan cheese. Bake for 10 minutes.

Serve hot. Nice as is, or under a ladleful of warm, seasoned tomato sauce.

SPANISH LENTIL SALAD

A summer dinner that crowns a bed of lettuce, and goes well with gazpacho. Serve with crusty bread.

SERVES 4

4 cups water
1½ cups brown or green lentils
1 bay leaf
1 small dried hot chili
1 T. cumin seeds

Bring water to the boil. Rinse lentils well and add with seasonings to boiling water. Cook for 45 minutes until tender. Skim off any foam that forms while boiling. Remove and discard bay leaf and chili. Drain the lentils. (Reserve liquid for soup stock, if desired.)

4 T. good quality olive oil
2 T. wine vinegar (or lemon juice)
1 bunch green onions, diced
1 cup corn kernels, thawed
2 to 3 cloves garlic, minced
1 small red bell pepper, minced
1 T. oregano
salt, pepper to taste

While lentils are still hot, toss with oil, vinegar, and seasonings. Let cool for at least one hour (or refrigerate and marinate overnight).

tomato wedges

Serve cool or at room temperature in a flat dish surrounded by fresh tomato wedges.

This dish is speedily assembled if you use canned or leftover cooked lentils. Black-eyed peas make a delicious variation. (Remember that black-eyed peas need between 1 and 1½ hours cooking time.)

NASI GORENG

*An Indonesian rice and tofu dish flavoured with cashews and cilantro.
Nasi Goreng is one of many lovely dishes that my friend Ilse Turnsen
has shared with me. Serve with vegetables and
a platter of sliced melon.*

2½ cups water
1 t. salt
1¼ cups brown rice

Bring salted water to the boil in a 2 quart pot. Add rice; return to the boil. Reduce heat and simmer, covered, for 45 minutes, until rice is tender and water has evaporated.

3 T. oil
2 medium onions, diced
6 cloves garlic, minced
½ to 1 t. crushed dried hot chilis
1 block tofu, pressed, drained, and crumbled
1 cup cashews
1 cup dried apricots, chopped
pepper to taste

While the rice is cooking, heat oil in a very large skillet or wok. Sauté onion, garlic, tofu, nuts, apricots, and seasonings until the onions are golden brown.

½ cup fresh cilantro, minced
¼ cup tamari

Add to onions; stir until heated throughout. Add to the cooked rice, stirring to combine thoroughly. Cover and let rest for 20 minutes. Serve warm. Nasi Goreng improves in flavour the following day.

MEDITERRANEAN PILAF

You can practically taste the warmth and sunshine
of the Mediterranean in this savoury delight.
Serve with Devilled Cauliflower, p. 103, and sliced tomatoes.

SERVES 4

2 T. olive oil
1 large onion, diced
4 cloves garlic, minced
1 (12 oz.) jar marinated artichoke
    hearts, drained* and chopped
½ cup sun-dried tomatoes, diced
1 small zucchini, diced
2 T. dried oregano
salt, pepper to taste

Heat oil in a skillet, and sauté onions and garlic until browned. Add artichoke hearts, tomatoes, zucchini, and seasonings. Sauté for another 5 minutes. Set aside.

3 T. olive oil
1¼ cups bulghar wheat
dash of salt
1 cup pine nuts

PREHEAT OVEN TO 375° F. In an ovenproof/stovetop casserole, heat oil and sauté the bulghar with salt and pine nuts until golden brown, stirring often.

2½ cups boiling water
1 bay leaf
½ cup lemon juice
1 T. dried mint

Add boiling water and remaining ingredients to sautéed bulghar in the casserole. Stir in the cooked vegetables; mix well. Cover and bake for 30 minutes. Stir twice while baking. Serve hot. Leftovers make an excellent cold salad.

---

* Slice an English cucumber, or steam some carrots, and marinate overnight in the refrigerator in the liquid drained from the artichoke hearts: a tangy companion to pasta.

BRAZILIAN PEANUT STEW

*An unusual combination of ingredients reflecting the
diversity of Brazil. Black beans swim in a heady
sauce of tomatoes, coconut and peanuts.*

SERVES 4

4 T. oil
1 T. achiote (annato seeds) or
   paprika
2 small dried hot chilis
1 large onion, chopped
4 cloves garlic, minced

Heat oil in a heavy-bottomed pot over medium high heat with achiote or paprika and dried chilis. (Remember to lower the heat with paprika, which scorches easily.) Once the oil is hot and has absorbed the flavours (3 to 5 minutes), remove and discard the seeds and chilis. Sauté onions and garlic in the flavoured oil until translucent.

1 (28 oz.) can tomatoes
1" cinnamon stick (or ¼ t. ground
   cinnamon)
1 T. grated fresh ginger
(or ¼ t. powdered ginger)
Grated nutmeg, cayenne pepper, salt,
   pepper to taste
1 cup water or vegetable broth
1 small bunch mint leaves, well-
   rinsed, trimmed, and chopped
   (optional)

Add tomatoes, seasonings, and liquid to the pot. Simmer over medium-high heat, stirring occasionally, for 15 to 20 minutes. Remove and discard cinnamon stick.

CONTINUED

1 cup canned coconut milk
⅓ to ½ cup smooth peanut butter
1 cup cooked black beans
1 cup corn kernels

1 cup peanuts

Blend coconut milk and peanut butter together until smooth. Add to the stew, stirring to incorporate completely. Add cooked beans and corn; stir. Add more water or stock, if necessary, to obtain desired consistency. Taste and adjust seasonings. Simmer another 15 minutes to heat throughout. Serve hot over rice, garnished with a generous sprinkling of peanuts.

MOROCCAN COUSCOUS

*The tantalizing scents of cinnamon, bay leaf, and apricot will
set your mouth watering when you lift the lid on this
North African classic. Serve with
Pistachio Honey-Glazed Carrots, p. 31.*

SERVES 4

3 cups water
½ cup diced dried apricots
½ cup raisins
⅓ cup minced fresh parsley
1 t. salt
1 bay leaf
1" cinnamon stick
1 pinch saffron

Place water, fruit, and
seasonings in a heavy 4 quart
pot. Cover and bring to the
boil.

1¼ cups couscous

Place couscous in a dry cast-
iron skillet over high heat.
Toast for 5 minutes, stirring
constantly, until golden brown;
avoid scorching. Add the
toasted grain to the boiling
water; stir well. Reduce heat to
low, cover, and let the couscous
cook for 10 to 15 minutes. The
grain will be tender and fluffy.

4 T. olive oil
1 cup diced onion
1 cup diced celery
1 cup frozen peas
2 cloves garlic, minced
½ cup almond slivers
pinch of hot dried chilis
salt, pepper to taste

Sauté vegetables, nuts and
seasonings together in oil.
When onions are tender, toss
the mixture gently with cooked
couscous. Mix well. Serve warm.

Leftovers make a delectable sandwich: stuff the couscous into
a pita pocket lined with lettuce.

THREE BEAN CHILI

Three colours of bean in authentic chili sauce:
serve this robust bean stew over rice, cornbread,
or bulghar. Freezes well. Leftovers heat up
beautifully for working lunches.

SERVES 4, WITH LEFTOVERS

4 cups water
¾ cup each pinto beans, kidney
    beans, and black beans
1 bay leaf
1 small hot dried chili
1" cinnamon stick

Bring water to the boil in a large pot with a heavy bottom. Rinse beans; drain; add to the pot. Remove from heat and soak for 1 hour. Add seasonings. Return to the boil and simmer for 2 hours, adding more water as needed to keep beans covered.

1 ½ cups water
6 large dried mild chilis, stems and
    seeds removed
1 (28 oz.) can tomatoes

Bring water to the boil in a skillet. Add chilis; boil for 5 minutes until softened. Add tomatoes; boil for another 5 minutes. Purée in a food processor or blender until smooth. Set aside.

2 T. oil
2 medium onions, chopped
6 cloves garlic, minced
2 stalks celery, diced
1 green bell pepper, chopped
1 red bell pepper, chopped
1 T. oregano
1 T. ground cumin
salt, pepper, Tabasco to taste

Heat oil in skillet. Sauté vegetables for 10 minutes with seasonings. Pour the blended chili liquid into skillet. Simmer for 10 minutes. Add the sautéed vegetables and chili sauce to the beans; stir well. Simmer 20 more minutes, or until beans are tender. Serve hot. Grated cheddar or Monterey Jack cheese makes an appetizing garnish.

CONTINUED

Look for mild dried chilis in the seasonings or produce section of your grocery store, or check a natural foods store or Latin American grocery. The dried chilis you want are mild, 2 to 4" in length, and a beautiful deep reddish brown. They may be called anaheim, ancho, New Mexico, or poblano peppers. It's important to buy mild, rather than hot chilis for this recipe.

With canned or leftover beans, this recipe comes together in a flash.

MACARONI MOUSSAKA

*A layered noodle casserole that melds the best of macaroni-n-cheese
with the lush richness of moussaka, the ever-popular Greek standby.*

8 cups water
3 cups raw macaroni noodles
2 t. salt (optional)

Bring salted water to the boil in a 3 quart pot. Add macaroni and boil for 12 minutes, until pasta is barely tender. Drain pasta and set aside in a large mixing bowl. PREHEAT OVEN TO 350° F.

2 T. olive oil
2 T. flour
2 cups yogurt
2 cloves garlic, minced
1 T. oregano
salt, pepper to taste
2 cups grated cheddar cheese (1 cup
    for sauce + 1 cup set aside for
    topping)

While the pasta is cooking, make the sauce. In a small bowl, whisk together flour, oil, yogurt, garlic, seasonings, and one cup of cheese. Add to cooked pasta; stir well, until pasta is thoroughly coated. Spread half the pasta evenly over the bottom of an oiled 9 x 13" pan.

2 medium zucchini, thinly sliced
1 large tomato, thinly sliced
½ cup pitted olives, chopped
1 medium onion, sliced in thin
    crescents
⅔ cup feta cheese, crumbled
    (optional)
2 T. basil
1 T. oregano
1 T. mint
1 t. pepper

Spread vegetables and herbs, olives, and cheese evenly over the layer of pasta. Top with the remaining pasta and sauce. Sprinkle with the remaining grated cheese and paprika or oregano for colour. Bake 35 minutes: covered for the first 20 minutes and uncovered for the last 15 minutes. Serve hot, with a salad.

BRAM BORA'K

A savoury baked potato pancake from Czechoslovakia.

SERVES 4

1 medium onion, finely chopped
3 cloves garlic, minced
1 large egg
⅓ cup flour
1 T. marjoram
¼ cup chopped fresh parsley (or 2 T. dried)
salt, pepper to taste

Combine ingredients thoroughly in a large mixing bowl. PREHEAT OVEN TO 425° F.

3 large potatoes, scrubbed or peeled (or 3 cups grated)

Sour cream or apple sauce for garnish, if desired

Grate the potatoes through the large holes of a hand grater or food processor. Drain in a sieve, using your hand or the back of a spoon to express as much liquid as possible. Work quickly to prevent the potatoes from browning in the air. Stir the drained potatoes into the egg mixture. Oil a 9" cast-iron skillet, or other ovenproof dish. Press the potato-egg mixture evenly over the pan. Bake for 20 to 25 minutes, or until potatoes are tender and the crust is crisp. Serve steaming hot. Sour cream and apple sauce are traditional condiments.

MEXICAN GREENS WITH POTATOES AND GARBANZOS

A hearty marriage of potatoes, garbanzo beans, and garden greens in a mildly spicy sauce. Make it the day before to integrate the flavours.

SERVES 4

6 cups water
8 medium red new potatoes
dash of salt

Bring salted water to the boil in a 3 quart pot. Rinse potatoes well and add them, whole, to the pot. Boil 15 to 20 minutes, until tender throughout. Drain and cut in quarters. Set aside.

2 T. oil
1 medium onion, chopped
4 cloves garlic, minced
½ t. dried crumbled hot chilis (or more to taste)
1 T. cumin
salt, pepper to taste
3 medium tomatoes, chopped
1 large bunch Swiss chard, rinsed, trimmed, and chopped
2 to 3 T. water

Sauté onions, garlic, and seasonings in a large skillet until tender. Add tomatoes, Swiss chard, and water. Reduce heat, cover, and simmer for 10 minutes, until chard is barely wilted.

1 cup cooked, drained garbanzo beans (chick peas)

Add cooked potatoes and garbanzos to the skillet. Stir well; simmer only until thoroughly heated. Serve hot, with rice on the side, or use tortillas to roll up spoonfuls of the potato mixture.

Red chard, green chard, spinach or collard greens are excellent choices for this recipe.

ACORN SQUASH STUFFED WITH WILD RICE AND PECANS

A lovely vegetarian entrée at holiday gatherings. Sage,
apples, and pecans are reminiscent of Thanksgiving.

SERVES 4

2½ cups water
1 t. salt
¾ cup brown rice
½ cup wild rice

PREHEAT OVEN TO 350° F. Bring salted water to the boil; add rice and return to the boil. Reduce heat to low, cover, and simmer for 45 minutes until rice is tender and water has evaporated. Set aside.

2 medium acorn squash

While the rice is cooking, prepare the squash. Trim the ends and cut each squash in half. Scrape out and discard the seeds; lightly salt and pepper the cavities. Invert the squash onto an oiled baking sheet, cut side down, tucking a slice of apple and green onion into each cavity. Bake for 15 to 20 minutes, until barely tender throughout. Remove from oven and set aside; leave oven on.

3 T. oil
½ cup sliced mushrooms
½ cup chopped pecans
1 carrot, finely diced
1 apple, finely diced
4 green onions, diced
¼ cup white wine
½ cup fresh parsley, minced
1 T. sage
1 T. lemon juice
½ t. nutmeg
salt, pepper to taste

Heat oil in a wok or skillet. Sauté vegetables and seasonings together until just barely tender. Mix with cooked rice until thoroughly integrated. Turn baked squash halves upright on baking sheet; stuff with rice mixture, heaping to form a neat mound. Bake for 10 to 15 minutes. Garnish with pecan halves or parsley sprigs, and serve hot.

TZIMMES

A vegetarian version of my grandmother's recipe.
This traditional Jewish holiday dish has an
intriguing savoury/sweet edge.

SERVES 4

1 block tofu, pressed and drained
3 T. tamari

Cut the tofu into 1" cubes and marinate in the tamari. Set aside. PREHEAT OVEN TO 300° F.

3 large potatoes
2 large carrots
1 cup dried prunes, cut in half

Cut vegetables in 1" cubes. Mix with prunes in an ovenproof casserole with a lid.

¾ cup catsup
salt, pepper to taste
1 T. apple cider vinegar
1 T. molasses
1½ cups water

Stir together liquid ingredients and combine with vegetables. Bake, covered, for 50 minutes.

2 sweet potatoes, cubed

½ cup fresh parsley, minced

Stir sweet potatoes and marinated tofu gently into casserole. Bake, covered, for another 15 to 20 minutes until vegetables are tender. Remove from oven and gently stir in the parsley. Serve hot.

SPAGHETTI

*One reliable cure for a broken heart, spaghetti. My vegetarian tomato
sauce is made with bulghar wheat, which gives it the hearty texture
reminiscent of a meat sauce, minus the cholesterol.*

SERVES 4

3 T. olive oil
2 medium onions, chopped
1 green pepper, chopped
4 or 5 cloves garlic, minced
1 cup sliced mushrooms
4 cups seasoned tomato sauce
   (see p. 199)
1 cup water

Heat oil in a heavy-bottomed
pot. Sauté onions, pepper, and
garlic until lightly browned,
adding mushrooms for the final
3 minutes. Add tomato sauce
and water; stir well. Heat over
medium high heat until sauce is
hot, stirring often.

½ cup bulghar wheat
1 t. salt
1 T. basil
2 t. oregano

Add bulghar and seasonings to
the sauce, and stir well. Reduce
heat, and simmer for about 20
minutes, until the accompanying
pasta is *al dente.*
Stir occasionally. (The bulghar
will continue to absorb liquid
from the sauce, so add small
quantities of water and adjust
seasonings as needed.)

12 cups water
8 oz. dried spaghetti
pinch of salt
splash of oil

While the tomato sauce is
simmering, bring water to the
rolling boil in a large pot. Add
pasta, oil, and salt. Stir
occasionally. Cook over high
heat at a rolling boil until pasta
is tender, about 12 minutes.
Drain pasta, and serve hot on
warmed plates. Ladle tomato
sauce over each serving of
cooked pasta.

PASTA CARBONARA

A generous dusting of fresh black pepper looks like coal dust, so Italians name this pasta dish carbonara. Quick and easy to make; but you have to move quickly once the pasta is ready.

12 cups water
8 oz. dried spaghetti
pinch of salt
splash of oil

Bring water to a rolling boil in a large pot. Add pasta, oil, and salt. Stir occasionally. Cook over high heat until the pasta is *al dente*, about 12 minutes.

4 T. oil
1 cup diced onions
4 cloves garlic, minced
1 T. dried basil
2 T. wine vinegar
½ cup diced zucchini
½ cup broccoli florets
½ cup sliced mushrooms
salt to taste

While waiting for the water to boil, prepare the vegetables. Heat oil in a large skillet. Sauté onion and garlic with vinegar, salt, and basil until translucent. Add zucchini, broccoli, and mushrooms. Sauté for a further 5 to 10 minutes. Set aside.

2 eggs, lightly beaten
⅓ cup Parmesan cheese

Timing is crucial at this point. Set out a large serving bowl and place the beaten eggs and cheese close at hand. Once vegetables are sautéed and the pasta is tender, drain the pasta;

CONTINUED

freshly ground black pepper

IMMEDIATELY mix in the eggs and cheese. Then stir in the vegetables. The heat of the just-boiled pasta cooks the eggs; you must move quickly to prevent a runny sauce. (If this happens, put the pasta back in the pot and heat it gently over medium low heat until the eggs are set. But it's much simpler to move quickly in the first place.) Stir well and serve hot, smothered with black pepper.

My favourite pasta dish, carbonara is very easy and quick to make, ready just minutes after the spaghetti is judged al dente. A package of pasta and a couple of eggs are almost always lurking around, even in otherwise bare cupboards. And leftovers taste delicious cold the next day. What more could you ask of a recipe?!

Note: other vegetables (carrots, green or red peppers, asparagus, tomatoes, green onions, etc.) substitute nicely. Or leave out all the vegetables, and serve the pasta with a large salad.

QUICK MEALS

There are nights or lunchtimes, when you just don't have the time or energy to fix a "real" meal. The next few recipes will provide inspiration for those times when you don't want to take time — each of the following recipes takes 30 minutes or less to prepare.

QUESADILLAS

*Tortilla triangles oozing with spicy melted cheese, ready to be
dipped in guacamole. Serve with refried beans and shredded
lettuce on the side, for a fast, satisfying dinner.*

SERVES 1, MULTIPLY AS NEEDED

1 T. butter or oil
4 flour tortillas
⅓ cup grated cheddar cheese
2 green onions, diced
1 or 2 T. picante sauce
salt, pepper to taste
fresh cilantro leaves (optional)

Heat butter or oil in a skillet.
Place one tortilla in the skillet.
Sprinkle with half the cheese,
half the diced onion, picante
sauce, and seasonings to taste.
When the cheese has melted
and the tortilla is lightly
browned, cover with another
tortilla to form a sandwich. Flip
to brown the second side.
Remove from heat; cut the
sandwich into quarters with a
large sharp knife. Keep warm in
a low oven (if you have lots to
cook, two skillets will speed up
the process).

Arrange the quesadilla quarters
on a plate with refried beans on
the side, shredded lettuce, and
diced tomatoes. Serve with
guacamole and/or sour cream
for dipping.

CONTINUED

TO MAKE GUACAMOLE:

 Select 1 or more ripe avocados. Peel; remove the pit. Mash thoroughly with a fork or in a food processor. Mix with a few tablespoons of sour cream or yogurt, hot sauce to taste, a dash of Worchestershire sauce, a generous squeeze of lime or lemon, salt and pepper to taste. If you're feeling generous, add diced green onions, diced tomatoes, cumin, and fresh cilantro as desired.

Ripe avocados are slightly firm, but they give to the touch; they should not be rock-like, nor blackened, nor mushy. If an avocado is not ripe when you buy it, speed the process by putting it in a paper bag, rolling the top of the bag securely shut, and placing in a sunny window for 2 or 3 days.

MINI-PIZZAS

Fast treats.

ALLOW 1 TO 2 PIZZAS PER PERSON. FOR EACH PIZZA:

pita bread
   or
kaiser roll, halved
   or
english muffin, halved
3 to 4 T. seasoned tomato sauce
   (your favourite brand, or make
   your own: p. 199)

Spread bread thinly and evenly
with tomato sauce.
PREHEAT OVEN TO 400° F.

TOPPINGS:

sliced onions
   and/or
sliced mushrooms
   and/or
pine nuts
   and/or
diced tomato
   and/or
diced green pepper
   and
mozzarella, grated
   and
parmesan cheese

Layer your choices evenly over
the tomato sauce, ending with
cheese. Bake for 10 minutes.

NACHOS

A great fast snack when the gang comes over, nachos can be as simple as cheese-on-corn chips, or as elaborate as your imagination allows.

SERVES 2 FOR DINNER, 4 FOR A SNACK

8 oz. corn tortilla chips (rounds or triangles)

1 to 2 cups grated cheese (medium cheddar or Monterey Jack)

4 to 6 T. picante sauce (mild, medium or hot, to taste)

PREHEAT OVEN TO 400° F. On a baking sheet with a rim, lay out the chips evenly. Add toppings (see below). Sprinkle cheese to cover the chips, and then spoon picante sauce over the cheese. Bake for 5 to 10 minutes, until cheese has completely melted. Serve immediately at a table where everyone can gather around and dig in.

TOPPINGS:

1 cup cooked pinto beans, well-drained

or spoonfuls of mashed pinto beans (refritos)

jalapeno peppers, diced or rings (fresh or canned)

diced tomatoes

diced onions or green onions

diced green peppers

diced canned green chilis

corn kernels

fresh cilantro, minced

garlic, minced

sprinkle of chili powder

a squeeze of lime juice

If you choose to use any (or all!) of these toppings in your quest for the ultimate nacho, then add them evenly over the corn chips, **before** you add the cheese, which must go on last.

(Warning: fully-loaded nachos are not a tidy dining experience.)

CONTINUED

Nachos are a favorite snack food of mine. I love the crunch of the chips, the ooey-gooey richness of the cheese, the bite of hot sauce, the pungent freshness of cilantro. With a simple salad, nachos provide a quick pick-me-up dinner at the end of a long day. And nachos made at home are a far cry from the stale chips and microwaved Velveeta that parade as nachos at fast-food stands.

BROILED STUFFED TOMATOES

Colourful pockets of flavour for a speedy,
appetizing summer supper.

SERVES 4

1 ½ cups boiling water
¾ cup couscous

Add couscous to boiling water; stir. Cover and let stand for 10 minutes.

½ cup frozen peas
½ cup sliced almonds
2 T. olive oil
1 T. balsamic or wine vinegar
1 T. basil
2 t. marjoram
salt, pepper to taste

Mix peas, almonds, and seasonings thoroughly with cooked couscous, fluffing with a fork. Cover to keep warm. PREHEAT BROILER OF OVEN AND PLACE OVEN RACK 8-10" FROM ELEMENT.

4 large tomatoes

4 T. almond slivers, or bread crumbs or paprika (as a garnish)

Slice off the tops of the tomatoes. If necessary, slice a very thin layer from their bottoms, so that the tomatoes sit flat. With a melon baller or sharp knife, carefully hollow out the centres of the tomatoes. Be careful not to cut through their skins at any point. Divide the couscous filling into 4 portions; stuff the hollowed-out tomatoes with couscous. Place on a lightly oiled pan with a rim. Broil 5 to 10 minutes. Watch closely to prevent burning, and turn the pan as necessary to cook evenly. For the final 2 minutes of broiling, sprinkle tomatoes with the garnish of your choice. Serve hot.

TEXAS TACO SALAD

All the best features of a taco, but easier to eat.

1 good-sized head of lettuce, shredded
1 cup cooked pinto or kidney beans,
    drained
1 cup corn kernels
1 cup cheddar cheese, grated
1 ripe avocado, sliced into wedges
4 green onions, diced

Divide the ingredients among 4 individual salad bowls. Layer in the following order: lettuce as a base, beans, corn, cheese, avocado slices, green onions.

¼ cup lime juice
1 clove garlic, minced
2 T. oil
1 T. chili powder
salt, pepper to taste

Whisk dressing ingredients together. Shake well; drizzle over each salad.

6 T. sour cream
4 to 8 T. picante sauce
2 medium tomatoes, sliced into wedges
1 pkg. of corn tortilla chips

Top each serving with a spoonful of picante sauce and a dollop of sour cream. Arrange tomato wedges and corn chips around each serving. Pass extra chips in a basket, and picante sauce.

BAKER'S DOZEN SANDWICH SUGGESTIONS

Bored with tuna fish sandwiches? Can't imagine what to put in a meat-free lunch box? Well, keep reading: the sandwiches suggested below may make you the envy of the brown-bag crowd.

SANDWICH:	FILLING:	BREAD:
1) Almond Joy	almond butter apple butter grated carrots and/or apple slices	raisin bread
2) Californian	avocado slices lettuce tomato slices sprouts picante sauce	whole wheat
3) PB & B	peanut butter banana slices honey cinnamon	whole wheat
4) Middle Eastern	hummus (garlicky chick pea spread) cucumber slices alfalfa sprouts tomato slices	pita pocket: open up the pita and stuff
5) Ruebenesque	Swiss cheese sauerkraut hot mustard black pepper	dark rye
6) BBQ Tofu	sliced barbequed tofu (see p. 28) extra BBQ sauce tomato slices onion slices	whole wheat bun
7) Burrito Roll-Ups	refried beans (canned, or see p.106) grated cheddar diced tomatoes and onion picante sauce	spread on a flour tortilla and roll into a cigar shape

SANDWICH:	FILLING:	BREAD:
8) Greek	pitted black olives crumbled feta cheese cucumber slices shredded lettuce tomato slices olive oil pepper	pita pocket: open up and stuff
9) Egg-straordinary	Curried Egg Salad (see p. 162) mayo mustard lettuce tomato slices	English muffin
10) Vegetable Hero	Swiss cheese grated carrot tomato slices red onion slices lettuce alfalfa sprouts hard-boiled egg, sliced fresh dill mayo mustard	long roll, sliced in half and piled high
11) Oasis	cashew butter apricot jam	nut bread

12) I Love Olives	cream cheese
	  mashed with
	    pitted,chopped
	    Calamata olives
	lettuce
	tomato slices
	dijon mustard
		onion bagel,
		split in half

13) Bombay Bagel	cream cheese cucumber slices chutney	sesame bagel, split in half

POPEYE'S FAVOURITE GRILLED CHEESE SANDWICH

Popeye's answer to any crisis...

2 slices dark rye bread
dijon mustard
2 thick slices Swiss or gruyère or
    cheddar cheese
4 to 6 fresh spinach leaves, trimmed,
    well-rinsed, and dried
2 tomato slices
pinch of nutmeg
pinch of black pepper

butter or oil

Generously spread bread with mustard, then layer with cheese, spinach leaves, and tomato slices. Sprinkle with pepper, dust lightly with nutmeg.

Heat butter or oil in a heavy skillet or griddle. Panfry sandwich on both sides until golden brown. Serve immediately.

161

CURRIED EGG SALAD

Popular as a sandwich spread or mounded on celery.
For a cholesterol-free variation, substitute one 8 oz.
block of tofu (pressed and drained) for the eggs.

MAKES ENOUGH FOR 4 SANDWICHES

6 hard-boiled eggs, peeled
½ cup plain yogurt

Mash the eggs and yogurt together with a potato masher or in a food processor.

1 T. oil
1 medium onion, finely diced
2 t. turmeric
1 t. coriander
¼ t. dried mustard
dash of cinnamon
dash of cayenne
salt, pepper to taste

Heat oil in a small skillet. Sauté the onion with seasonings until translucent. Set aside to cool.

2 green onions, diced
½ cup diced cucumber

Combine eggs, onions, and cucumber. Mix well. Flavour improves overnight. Store in a sealed container in the refrigerator.

TO HARDBOIL EGGS:

Place eggs in a pot just large enough that the eggs are not crowded on top of each other. Cover the eggs with cool water. Add 1 t. cider vinegar. Place over high heat and bring to the boil. When the water comes to a boil, start the timer: boil the eggs for 10 minutes. After 10 minutes, remove from heat and immediately run cold water over the eggs. When they are cool enough to handle, drain; then peel. Rinse the peeled eggs free of shell fragments. There's a reason for adding the eggs before you boil the water: they're less likely to crack. The vinegar makes the eggs easier to peel.

BAKING,
BREAKFASTS, &
BRUNCH TREATS

Around the same time every day, Winnie the Pooh was struck by the need for "a little something." While a fictional character — and a bear of very little brain besides — I think he was on to something important. For Pooh that Something was honey, which I use as the primary sweetener for baked goods.

It is essentially unfair, I feel, that sweet things are good neither for our bodies nor our teeth. Sweet things have always been, and likely always will be, a great weakness of mine. I refrain from them when I can, which isn't really all that often. I try to make the ones that I bake at home a little healthier by using honey instead of the more refined white sugar, and by mixing in some whole wheat flour with the white. But I firmly believe that if you're going to eat a dessert, it should seem like a dessert and not a penance, heavy and hard. So these baked goods are relatively light and sweet, a trade-off between what's good for you and what's good to eat. If you feel the need to make the recipes "healthier" yet, then bake with whole wheat flour exclusively, or use less honey. You'll need to adjust proportions of other ingredients, since healthier baking ingredients tend to change the texture of the finished product.

I've included recipes for muffins and quick breads, coffee cakes, fruit pies, and a truly wonderful concoction called "Breakfast Pizza." All these recipes are easy and relatively failproof. I know this because I'm a bad-tempered, impatient baker (as my baking friends will testify), and I can make these recipes.

Brunch is one of my favourite meals. All the components are attractive: sleeping late, a leisurely schedule, several sweet carbohydrate-happy baked goods and classical music in the background. Invite friends over to share and you've got the makings for a lovely meal and a good day. I've included recipes for some of my "personal best" brunch treats, as well as a couple of suggestions for those workaday breakfasts that lack the leisure time to be designated brunch.

YOGURT & HERB SCONES

A scrumptious quickbread to serve with soups.

SERVES 6

2 cups flour (all white, or half whole
    wheat or durum)
1 t. dried basil or tarragon or dill
2 T. baking powder
½ t. salt

PREHEAT OVEN TO 400° F, and lightly grease a cookie sheet.

¼ cup cold butter or stick margarine,
    cut into little cubes

Combine dry ingredients in a bowl. Cut in butter cubes with a pastry cutter or work the mix with your fingertips until crumbly.

2 eggs
⅔ cup lowfat yogurt

In a separate bowl or 2-cup measuring cup, beat together eggs and yogurt. Pour into dry ingredients and stir briefly with a fork or spatula. Do not overmix.

Turn out dough on a greased baking sheet. Flour the palms of your hands and pat the dough into a circle about ½" thick. Bake for 12 minutes, or until a toothpick poked in the centre of the scone comes out clean. Cut into wedges and serve warm.

QUICK OAT BREAD

Fast, easy, and wheat-free; scrumptious with soups, salads or brunches.
This bread is best served warm from the oven,
capped with butter, apple butter, or strawberry jam.

YIELD: ONE 9" PAN

2 cups quick-cooking oats
4 t. baking powder
¾ t. salt
2 eggs
½ cup raisins
⅓ cup honey
½ t. vanilla extract
¾ cup orange juice or apple juice or
    milk

PREHEAT OVEN TO 400° F.
Combine all ingredients except
the oil together with a few
quick strokes.

4 T. vegetable oil

Heat 2 T. oil in a 9" ovenproof
skillet (cast-iron works well).
Pour the batter over the hot oil.
Spread remaining 2 T. oil over
the top of the batter.

Bake for 20 to 25 minutes.
Remove to a plate to cool for
several minutes, and cut in
wedges. This bread is best the
day it is made (but it's so good
that it hardly ever makes it to a
second day!).

CONTINUED

This bread is extremely versatile…add nuts or dried fruits, cinnamon, nutmeg, or vanilla; I've sweetened it with apple butter when I was out of honey. I've even enjoyed it when the oven blew a fuse halfway through baking; the ingenious cook steamed it, covered, on top of the stove!

You can make a savoury version that's very satisfying with bean or pea soup. Substitute milk or soymilk for the juice; omit the raisins, honey and vanilla; add one cup finely diced onions, and a handful of minced fresh herbs (parsley, chives, or basil), and a pinch of black pepper; bake as directed.

CORNBREAD

This humble but loveable quickbread is a Southern tradition.
Good company for chili, soup, black-eyed peas, and gumbo.

¾ cup whole wheat flour
1¼ cups cornmeal
1 T. baking powder
1 t. salt

PREHEAT OVEN TO 400° F. Mix dry ingredients together in a large mixing bowl.

1 egg
1 cup milk
2 T. honey

Beat together in a small bowl until thoroughly mixed. Add to dry ingredients, stirring with a fork until just mixed.

2 T. oil

Pour oil into 8" pan (a cast-iron skillet works best) and heat in oven. (Preheating the oiled pan in this way makes for a better crust.) When oil is hot, tilt pan so that the oil coats sides and bottom. Drain the oil into the cornbread batter. Stir briefly. Pour batter into hot pan. Bake for 25 minutes, or until toothpick inserted in the centre comes out clean.

Double this recipe to fill a 9 x 13" pan. Jazz it up with well-drained corn kernels, grated cheese, canned diced green chilis, or jalapeños…see Sage Corn Muffins, p. 169.

If you use a glass or Pyrex baking dish, remember to lower the oven temperature by 25 degrees.

SAGE CORN MUFFINS

A southwestern twist on cornbread. Make these muffins whenever you can get fresh sage.

YIELD: 12 MUFFINS

¾ cup whole wheat or corn flour
1¼ cups cornmeal
1 T. baking powder
1 t. salt
½ t. pepper

PREHEAT OVEN TO 400° F. Mix dry ingredients together in a large mixing bowl.

1 egg
1 cup milk
1 T. honey

Beat together in a small bowl until thoroughly mixed. Add to dry ingredients, stirring with a fork until just mixed.

2 T. oil
2 cloves garlic, minced
2 T. fresh sage, minced
(or 1 ½ t. dried)

Sauté garlic and sage in a small pan. Add to batter; stir briefly. Pour batter into oiled muffin tins. Bake for 15 minutes or until a toothpick inserted in the centre comes out clean.

SHEILA'S SESAME OAT CRACKERS

Crispy homemade oat crackers with the taste of sesame, great with cheese or tofu dips, or with soups.

MAKES 24 CRACKERS

⅔ cup flour
½ t. baking soda
½ cup sesame seeds
½ cup oats
½ cup oat bran

PREHEAT OVEN TO 400° F. Mix dry ingredients in a bowl.

½ cup tahini (sesame butter)
1 egg
3 T. toasted sesame oil
1 T. tamari
2 to 4 T. milk

Mix wet ingredients except for milk in a small bowl. Add to dry and mix. Add just enough milk so that dough comes together. Drop by spoonfuls onto a cookie sheet and flatten with the floured bottom of a glass. Bake for 12 to 15 minutes until golden brown.

PUMPKIN GINGERBREAD

Two popular flavours in a dark, moist, spicy loaf.

YIELD: ONE 9" LOAF

¾ cup whole wheat flour
¾ cup white flour
1 ½ t. baking powder
1 t. baking soda
½ t. salt
1 t. cinnamon
¼ t. cloves
1 t. dried ginger

PREHEAT OVEN TO 350° F. Mix dry ingredients together in a large bowl.

¾ cup honey
3 T. molasses
½ cup oil
2 small eggs, beaten
1 cup mashed, cooked pumpkin or winter squash
½ cup walnut pieces
⅔ cup raisins

In a separate bowl, cream together the oil, honey, and molasses. Add eggs, one at a time. Add pumpkin, mixing well; stir in nuts and raisins.

Add to dry ingredients; mix thoroughly. Pour into a greased and floured loaf pan. Bake 75 to 90 minutes until done (when a toothpick inserted in the centre comes out clean).

Double this recipe to make 2 loaves at a time; freeze one for later use. Or pour the batter into mini-loaf pans to make several smaller loaves for gift-giving or freezing (smaller loaves will need less baking time). When bread has cooled completely, securely wrap inside double plastic bags to freeze.

COCONUT LOAF

This moist quickbread will fill your kitchen with the tropical fragrance of coconut and allspice.

YIELD: ONE 9" LOAF

1 cup white flour
1 cup whole wheat flour
½ T. baking powder
½ t. salt
2 cups coconut
1 t. nutmeg or mace
½ t. allspice

PREHEAT OVEN TO 325° F.
Mix together in a large bowl.

2 eggs
⅔ cup apple juice
½ t. vanilla extract
½ cup honey
½ cup sunflower or canola oil
⅔ cup chopped pitted dates
    (optional)
1 cup slivered almonds (optional)

In separate bowl, beat together wet ingredients. Add to dry ingredients, mixing thoroughly. Pour into a lightly oiled loaf pan. Bake for 30 minutes, or until a toothpick inserted in the centre comes out clean. Remove from loaf pan and cool on a wire rack.

CARROT PINEAPPLE MUFFINS

A moist, flavourful treat.

YIELD: 12 MUFFINS

⅓ cup oil
⅓ cup honey
2 eggs
½ cup crushed pineapple with juice
½ t. vanilla extract

1¼ cups whole wheat flour
1 T. baking powder
½ cup sunflower seeds
½ cup raisins (optional)
¼ cup wheat germ
¼ cup grated coconut
1¼ cups grated carrot

PREHEAT OVEN TO 400° F.
Combine wet ingredients in a large bowl, beating well.

Add remaining ingredients to batter, stirring until just combined. Divide into greased muffin tins. Bake 20 minutes, until golden brown. A toothpick inserted in the centre should come out clean.

MAPLE NUT MUFFINS

If you want to cut down on eggs, try these muffins. Tofu replaces the eggs in these no-cholesterol treats, perfected by Paula Ring. The texture is crumbly, the flavour is maple heaven.

YIELD: 12 MUFFINS

4 cups oats
2 cups flour
1 cup pecans or walnuts, chopped
2 T. baking powder
½ t. salt
1 t. cinnamon

PREHEAT OVEN TO 375° F.
Mix dry ingredients together in a large bowl.

1 block tofu, pressed and drained
1 cup sunflower oil
¾ cup maple syrup
1⅓ cups water

Blend tofu in a blender or food processor until very smooth. Add oil, maple syrup, and water: blend briefly, just until incorporated. Pour over the oats and stir briefly, just until blended. Bake in muffin tins lined with paper liners. (These muffins are very crumbly and need to be handled gently: the paper liners will make it easier to get them out of the pans without breaking). Bake for 20 minutes, rotating pan once while baking so that the muffins rise and brown evenly.

APPLE CRANBERRY PIE

The tartness of Granny Smith apples and cranberries is tamed by the golden sweetness of maple syrup...a scrumptious pie!

YIELD: ONE 9" PIE

1 recipe Open Sesame double pie
   crust, p. 176

Prepare dough and set to chill.

5 or 6 Granny Smith apples
1 cup chopped cranberries
½ cup maple syrup
1 t. nutmeg
1 t. cinnamon
pinch of cloves
pinch of salt
juice and zest of one lemon
2 T. flour
½ cup toasted walnuts (optional)

Mix filling ingredients together in a bowl. Toss gently until thoroughly mixed. Mound over the bottom pie crust; cover with top crust or latticework. Bake as directed in pastry recipe.

OPEN SESAME PIE CRUST

1 ½ cups oat flour*
½ cup sesame seeds*
½ t. salt
½ cup chilled butter or stick
    margarine, cut into small cubes
6 T. ice water

Combine flour, sesame seeds, and salt in a large bowl. Cut the butter cubes into the flour, using a pastry cutter, two knives, or your fingers. Add water a spoonful at a time, stirring with a fork until the dough comes together into a ball. Do not handle the dough any more than necessary, or it will toughen. Divide the dough in two equal portions. Wrap in plastic and chill for 30 minutes in the refrigerator.

PREHEAT OVEN TO 450° F. Roll out one ball of chilled dough onto a lightly floured surface. Line a 9" pie plate with the pastry, fitting it loosely into the plate and pressing to fit sides. Prick pastry with a fork. Fill the pie shell with fruit filling.

Roll out the remaining ball of dough; cut into strips to weave a lattice over the filling. (You may have some leftover pastry.) Crimp together the two crusts, pinching or scoring the edge. Trim excess. Bake for 10 minutes; REDUCE HEAT TO 350° and bake another 30 minutes, until crust is golden brown.

CONTINUED

* For enhanced flavour, toast the oat flour and the sesame seeds at 375 degrees for 10 minutes before use.

If you don't have oat flour, substitute 1 cup white flour and ½ cup whole wheat flour.

MOCHA BROWNIES

What cookbook would be complete without a brownie recipe?
Half-a-cuppa java perks up these dense, fudgey treats.

Yield: ONE 8" SQUARE PAN, OR 9 GENEROUS BROWNIES

½ cup butter or margarine
½ cup honey
½ cup brewed coffee
⅓ cup cocoa powder
1 t. cinnamon

Combine and cook in a small saucepan over medium heat for 5 minutes until smooth. Set aside to cool.

2 large eggs
1 t. vanilla extract

PREHEAT OVEN TO 350° F. In a large mixing bowl, beat eggs until pale and fluffy; slowly pour in the vanilla and cooled cocoa sauce.

½ cup white flour
½ cup whole wheat flour
½ cup chopped pecans

Combine dry ingredients. Add to the egg mixture, stirring until just combined. Do not overmix. Oil bottom only of an 8" square pan. Pour batter into pan and bake 20 minutes. Cool before cutting.

If you use a glass or Pyrex baking dish, reduce the temperature of the oven by 25 degrees.

BANANA-COCONUT PIE

A dreamy, no-bake banana filling in an easy crust.

SERVES 6 TO 8

2 cups graham cracker crumbs
⅓ cup butter melted with
1 T. honey

PREHEAT OVEN TO 350° F. Mix crumbs with butter and honey. Pat evenly over the sides and bottom of a deep dish 9" pie pan. Bake for 10 to 15 minutes, until crust is golden brown. Set aside to cool.

⅓ cup sour cream
⅓ cup lowfat yogurt
3 T. honey
½ t. nutmeg
4 large ripe bananas, sliced
½ cup shredded coconut soaked in
¼ cup orange juice
½ t. vanilla
3 to 4 T. toasted almond slivers

Combine yogurt, sour cream, honey, nutmeg, and vanilla. Gently stir in the fruit. Spoon into pie crust and spread evenly. Let chill for 2 to 3 hours; the filling will thicken. Serve chilled, garnished with almond slivers.

APPLE AND CHEDDAR COFFEECAKE

A delicious brunch cake.

Y̲IELD: ONE 9″ PAN

½ cup whole wheat flour
1 cup white flour
1 T. baking powder
2 t. cinnamon
½ t. salt
⅔ cup apple juice
2 T. sunflower oil
1 egg, beaten
3 T. honey

PREHEAT OVEN TO 375° F.
Combine ingredients with
whisk or electric mixer on low
speed until well mixed. Scrape
the sides of the bowl with a
spatula.

1 cup grated cheddar cheese (medium
  or sharp)
1 medium apple, chopped
½ cup chopped walnuts or toasted
  sunflower seeds

Stir remaining ingredients into
batter. Spread batter evenly into
an oiled 9″ pan. Bake for 20
minutes.

2 T. honey
1 T. apple juice
½ t. nutmeg
1 t. oil

Whisk together in a measuring
cup and drizzle over the cake.
Bake for another 5 to 10
minutes, or until a toothpick
inserted in the centre of the
cake comes out clean.

GINGERBREAD PANCAKES

These pancakes are among the best in the world, I think. They are adapted from a recipe featured at The Omelettry, a famous breakfast restaurant in Texas. A guaranteed cure-all for grumpiness or depression.

YIELD: 8 TO 10 HEFTY PANCAKES

3 *eggs*
2 *T. honey*
2 *T. molasses*

Beat together.

½ *cup yogurt*
½ to ⅔ *cup water or soymilk*
⅓ *cup brewed coffee*

Add to the eggs.

1 *cup white flour*
1 ½ *cups buckwheat or oat or whole wheat flour*
½ *t. salt*
1 *t. baking powder*
2 *t. baking soda*
1 *t. allspice or cloves*
1 *T. cinnamon*
1 *T. ground ginger*
1 *T. ground nutmeg*

In a separate bowl, combine all dry ingredients. Pour in the wet ingredients, mixing just enough to combine. DO NOT OVERMIX!

4 *T. sunflower or other light oil*

Add oil to the batter and stir briefly. Add more liquid by the spoonful if needed to thin the batter. Ladle or pour batter (about ⅓ cup of batter per pancake) onto a hot, lightly oiled griddle or nonstick skillet. When air bubbles have formed, and then burst, flip pancake to brown the other side. Do not flip again. Serve hot with butter, margarine, apple butter, yogurt, or syrup.

APPLE-CINNAMON YOGURT

A lovely breakfast, alone or over pancakes. This easy treat also makes a cooling side dish for Indian curries.

YIELD: 3 CUPS

2 cups lowfat yogurt 4 T. honey 2 t. cinnamon	Mix with a fork until thoroughly blended.
2 medium apples (Red Delicious, Macintosh or Granny Smith)	Rinse, core, and grate the apples by hand or with the grater of a food processor. Mix grated apple immediately with the yogurt to prevent discolouration. Store in the refrigerator, tightly sealed. Serve chilled.

METRIC/IMPERIAL CONVERSIONS

1 teaspoon (t.) = 5 millilitres (ml)
1 tablespoon (T.) = 15 millilitres (ml)
1 cup = approximately 250 ml
1 ounce (oz.) = approximately 30 grams
2.2 pounds (lbs.) = 1 kilogram
1 inch (") = 2.54 centimetres (cm)

BREAKFAST PIZZA

*Pizza for breakfast?! You bet! Colourful fruit layered
with cream cheese and jam on a tea biscuit crust...
Hold the anchovies!*

SERVES 4

1 cup white flour
½ cup whole wheat flour
1 T. baking powder
¾ t. salt
¼ cup cold butter or stick margarine
scant ⅔ cup milk
½ cup raisins

Combine dry ingredients in a large mixing bowl. Cut in butter with a pastry cutter or two knives until mixture is the consistency of cornmeal. Add milk and raisins all at once; stir briefly until the dough comes away from the sides of the bowl and holds together.

PREHEAT OVEN TO 450° F. Turn out dough onto a lightly floured board and knead 10 to 15 strokes. Place dough on an ungreased baking sheet. Using a floured hand, pat out the dough into a large, even circle, ⅔" thick. Bake for 12 to 15 minutes, until the pastry is cooked in the centre and golden brown. Remove from oven; cool slightly.

6 oz. cream cheese or low fat ricotta
or yogurt cheese, softened
strawberry jam or marmalade

Spread the cooled pastry evenly with softened cream cheese. Using a spatula, spread a layer of jam or marmalade over the cream cheese.

Assorted fruit (Strawberry halves, slices of kiwifruit, peeled sections of mandarin orange, slices of banana, slices of fresh peach, seedless grape halves, raspberries, etc.) rinsed and well-drained

Layer the sliced fruit attractively over the jam.

2 T. honey dissolved with 1 T. lemon juice

Drizzle the honey and lemon glaze over the fruit. Garnish the breakfast pizza with a sprig of mint. Slice into wedges to serve.

You can also make 4 individual mini-pizzas from this recipe.

MIGAS

Tex-Mex scrambled eggs with potatoes scrambled right in. Served wrapped in a tortilla, migas make a popular brunch or a simple supper. This easy dish always gets rave reviews, and goes well with corn-on-the-cob and fruit salad.

2 T. oil
1 cup cooked, diced potatoes
1 medium onion, diced
3 cloves garlic, minced
1 medium red or green bell pepper, diced
3 corn or flour tortillas, diced
1 large tomato, diced
2 t. chili powder
1 to 3 T. picante sauce
salt, pepper to taste

Heat oil in a large skillet. Over medium high heat, sauté onions, potatoes, and garlic for 5 minutes. Add peppers, tortilla pieces, tomatoes and seasonings. Sauté another 5 minutes.

8 eggs, beaten with
3 T. milk or water
1 cup grated cheddar cheese

Pour eggs into skillet; reduce heat to medium. Cook, uncovered, for 10 to 15 minutes, stirring often, until eggs are barely cooked (to your preference). Sprinkle cheese on top, cover and remove from heat for 5 minutes to melt cheese. Serve hot with extra warmed tortillas, salsa, and sour cream on the side.

Diced zucchini or mushrooms make a tasty addition. Sauté crumbled corn tortilla chips instead of tortilla pieces. If desired, add 1 fresh minced hot chili pepper, or fresh cilantro.

HOMEFRIES

Many people know home-fried potatoes as an essential component of a deluxe breakfast. But homefries are also wonderful with tomato soup, or next to a tofu burger or tofu "hot dog" from your natural foods store. Next time you feel the need for some comfort food, boil or bake a few spuds for a down-home treat.

SERVES 4

3 to 4 T. oil
1 medium onion, diced
2 cloves garlic, minced
4 cups cooked potatoes, peeled and
    cubed
salt, pepper to taste
1 T. dried parsley
1 t. paprika
1 t. marjoram (optional)
1 t. dill (optional)

Heat oil in a large cast- iron skillet. Sauté onion and garlic for several minutes until onions begin to brown. Add seasonings and cooked potatoes. Cook over medium heat until potatoes are browned and crisp on all sides (about 15 minutes). Flip potatoes frequently with a metal spatula, scraping the bottom of the skillet to loosen the delicious crust. Serve hot.

This humble dish becomes a gourmet treat with the addition of several tablespoons of fresh herbs: parsley, dill, or basil are excellent. Experiment with cilantro! For a Southwest-style side dish, sauté onions and boiled potatoes with chili powder and some roasted canned green chilis, coarsely diced.

HASHBROWNS

First cousin to home fries; this time the potatoes are grated. Nothing fancy, just diner-style satisfaction. Best if you precook the potatoes the night before, to give yourself a headstart on a great breakfast.

SERVES 4

3 large potatoes, scrubbed

Several hours (or the night before) put whole potatoes in a pot. Cover with water; bring to the boil. Remove from heat, and let stand for several hours. Precooking assures a good texture for the potatoes and makes them easier to fry.

1 medium onion, minced
salt, pepper to taste
4 T. oil

Grate the potatoes by hand or in a food processor. Heat oil in a cast-iron skillet. Add grated potatoes and onions, and spread out evenly over the pan. Season to taste. Brown on one side; reduce heat as needed to avoid burning. Flip with a metal spatula and brown on the second side. Eat immediately.

FRUITY HOT CEREAL

A delicious and nutrition-packed start to your day.

SERVES 4

3 cups lowfat milk or soymilk
¼ cup honey
¼ cup diced dried apricots
¼ cup raisins
1 medium apple, seeded and diced
⅓ cup sunflower seeds or nuts
dash of salt

Heat milk gently over medium heat until it simmers, without letting it boil. (A heat deflector ring under the pot is helpful.) Add fruits, nuts, honey, and salt. Stir to dissolve the honey.

1 cup bulghar wheat

Add bulghar to milk; stir. Simmer, covered, for 10 minutes over low heat, stirring occasionally. Uncover and cook 5 more minutes until the bulghar is tender and liquid is fully absorbed. Serve hot with a spoonful of butter, yogurt, honey, or jam.

FRUIT SALAD WITH POPPYSEED DRESSING

Chunks of fresh fruit glisten in a sweet, light dressing.

SERVES 4

¼ cup lemon juice
2 T. honey
½ t. mace or nutmeg
pinch of salt
½ cup sunflower or other light oil
2 T. poppyseeds

Blend lemon juice, honey, and seasonings. While whisking or blending, trickle in the oil in a slow steady stream. When dressing is completely blended, stir in the poppyseeds.

1 large apple, chopped
1 cup seedless grapes
½ canteloupe, seeded, peeled, and cut into cubes
2 bananas, peeled and thickly sliced
2 cups strawberries, halved
½ cup raisins

Prepare the fruit. Toss gently in a serving, until fruit is lightly coated with dressing. Fresh mint leaves make an attractive garnish.

Add or substitute honeydew melon, fresh pineapple, pitted cherries, peach or nectarine slices, kiwi, etc. Do not prepare fruit until the dressing is ready; apples and bananas will darken when exposed to air.

This dressing is lovely over a salad of romaine lettuce, slivers of red onion, and segments of seedless oranges.

FRUIT SLUSHIES

A cooling treat for kids and adults.

YIELD: 4 ONE-CUP SERVINGS

3 dozen ice cubes
1 cup frozen juice concentrate
(orange, apple, etc.)
squeeze of lemon juice
½ to 1 cup fruit juice or water

Drop ice cubes into a plastic bag; pound with a hammer to break the ice into smaller pieces (for easier blending). Place ice, frozen concentrate, and lemon juice in a blender. Process in short bursts, with the lid on, until ice is uniformly crushed. Add juice or water as needed to obtain desired consistency. Serve immediately in cups, with a spoon. Combine fruit juice flavours, or add whole strawberries or blueberries to the blender, for a pleasant variation.

CINNAMON COFFEE

A cup of this fragrant coffee with frothed milk makes an aromatic ending to a special dinner. (Also the best reason for getting out of bed in the morning.)

SERVES 4

4 heaping tablespoons ground coffee
 (or to taste)
1" cinnamon stick
⅓ t. vanilla extract
4 cups boiling water

If you have a drip or filter cone coffee maker, place ground coffee, cinnamon stick* and vanilla in the filter. Pour boiling water through the filter. Serve steaming hot, black or with frothed milk.

*Don't use ground cinnamon: the powdered spice will clog the filter.

1 cup lowfat milk

dash of cinnamon
dash of cocoa

Heat milk over medium heat while whipping with a whisk until very frothy. Pour into coffee, sprinkle with cinnamon and cocoa.

METRIC/IMPERIAL CONVERSIONS

1 teaspoon (t.) = 5 millilitres (ml)
1 tablespoon (T.) = 15 millilitres (ml)
1 cup = approximately 250 ml
1 ounce (oz.) = approximately 30 grams
2.2 pounds (lbs.) = 1 kilogram
1 inch (") = 2.54 centimetres (cm)

THE PANTRY

(A Selection of Convenience Foods and Sauces)

I've included several recipes that you can make yourself at home, which will take the place of store-bought convenience foods. Prepare these on an evening or weekend when you have the time, and enjoy them later. These recipes include several food items you can make and freeze or store in the fridge to have on hand for future use: tomato sauce, BBQ sauce, breadcrumbs, etc. It may not be as convenient as buying these products at the store, but it's certainly cheaper; you get control over the seasonings and salt, and you exclude the preservatives or dyes.

VEGETABLE STOCK

Vegetable broth or stock plays a critical role in vegetarian soups. In meat-based soups or stews, the meat itself makes the broth both rich and flavourful. Similarly, vegetable stock gives more flavour to soup than plain water. One very easy flavour-booster, which also supplies nutrients, is the reserved cooking water from boiled or steamed vegetables. Drain; cool; keep in a jar in the refrigerator for 3 to 4 days. Vegetable cooking water is excellent for flavouring rice or other grains, for cooking beans, or as soup stock.

A richer stock is easily made from vegetable ends and peels. Bring 8 or more cups of water to the boil in a large pot. For a green stock, rinse and add the ends or stems of celery, parsley, green beans, green onions, spinach, lettuce, or zucchini. For a stock that is richer in flavour and brown in colour, add carrot peels and the skins and ends of onions and garlic: altogether, 3 to 4 cups of clean vegetables, peels, or ends. Toss in a bay leaf, cracked peppercorns, and herbs. (Avoid cabbage, broccoli, cauliflower, or peppers, as these leave a strong or bitter flavour.) Potato peels make a cloudy, starchy stock, appropriate for potato or barley soups.

Boil the water and vegetables until the water is reduced by half. Discard the vegetables and strain the broth through a fine sieve. Use the broth as a base for soups or add to sauces. Stock will keep 3 to 4 days in an airtight container in the refrigerator. Or freeze the stock in ice-cube trays, then store the frozen broth cubes in a plastic bag in the freezer, thawing for use as needed.

READY-TO-USE GARLIC

Peel and mince an entire head or two of garlic...more if you're an alliophile (lover of garlic). A food processor saves time, but the job can be done with a sharp knife or a garlic press and some fortitude. Place minced garlic in a small jar with a wide mouth and a tight-fitting lid. Add enough sunflower, sesame, or canola oil to cover the minced garlic. Date the jar and tighten the lid; it will keep for several weeks in the fridge. This technique makes it extremely easy to spoon out small – or large! – amounts of ready-to-use garlic whenever you're whipping up something that calls for that heady taste. And the oil absorbs the garlic flavour, so pour off a tablespoon or two for an instant hit of garlic heaven in stirfrying or salad dressings. Top up the oil level as you use it, to keep the garlic covered.

FLAVOURED VINEGARS AND OILS

You can take the same technique, and branch out from the jar of garlic to make your own flavoured vinegars and oils. Decant any mild-flavoured oil into a clean jar with a closely-fitting lid: choose a jar that pours easily. Add any combination of the following: 2 or 3 sprigs of fresh tarragon, fresh rosemary, fresh dill, 1 or 2 whole dried chilis, 2 to 6 whole garlic cloves, basil leaves, 5 or 6 peppercorns, etc. Seal firmly and and store in a cool, dark location. This method works equally well with vinegar: use good quality white wine vinegar (red wine or cider vinegars confuse the flavouring).

Flavoured oils and vinegars improve with age. Most will keep for several months; discard after 6 months or at the first glimpse of mold. A delightful gift which bears your signature, flavoured vinegars and oils dress salads and jazz up vegetable stirfries at the drop of a hat.

HERBED BREADCRUMBS

*A bag of breadcrumbs kept in the freezer makes
an easy finish for casseroles.*

YIELD: 1 TO 1½ CUPS

6-8 slices stale bread, toasted or plain
pinch of oregano, sage, pepper

Break up bread or dry toast into chunks. Grind bread in food processor or blender with herbs, until reduced to fine crumbs. Use immediately, or store in the freezer.

Hint: Grind an entire loaf of bread at one sitting. Freeze in a large plastic bag, so that you can use a small portion whenever you need it.

SESAME SPRINKLE

Sprinkle the rich taste (not to mention the calcium and protein) of sesame over steamed vegetables or cooked grains, with this delectable Japanese condiment, called gomasio.

YIELD: 2 CUPS

2 cups sesame seeds
1 T. salt (or more to taste)

Heat a dry cast-iron skillet over medium high heat. Add sesame seeds and salt and cook until toasty brown, stirring frequently to prevent the seeds from burning.

When seeds are toasted, remove from heat and cool. Grind in food processor or (clean!) coffee bean grinder in short, controlled bursts only until the seeds have burst open. DO NOT OVERGRIND: the seeds must not become a paste. (It's also possible to grind the seeds with a mortar and pestle. The Japanese have designed a specially ridged bowl exclusively for this task.)

Store gomasio indefinitely, in an airtight container in the refrigerator. Sprinkle over cooked vegetables or grains and savour the delicious flavour.

BASIC TOMATO SAUCE

*A building-block recipe! Start with this basic
sauce and add the variations of your choice.*

4 T. olive oil
2 cups chopped onions
6 to 8 cloves garlic, minced

Heat oil in a large, heavy-bottomed pot. Sauté onions and garlic until translucent.

2 (28 oz.) cans tomatoes (or 6 cups
chopped fresh tomatoes)

Stir in tomatoes and continue to simmer. (If using canned tomatoes, drain and reserve juice; chop tomatoes coarsely and add to onions. Simmer 15 minutes, then add juice and continue cooking.)

2 to 3 t. dried crumbled hot chilis
1 bay leaf
2 T. dried basil
1 T. dried oregano
salt and pepper to taste
a very small dash of something sweet
dash of Worcestershire sauce
2 slices (¼" thick) fresh ginger

Add seasonings to tomato sauce and stir well. Add any variations from the list below; stir well and simmer. Continue to simmer over medium low heat for 30 to 90 minutes, stirring occasionally. The longer it simmers, the better the flavour. Be careful not to scorch the sauce. Remove and discard bayleaf and ginger slices.

VARIATIONS:
1 large green pepper, chopped
1 bunch green onions, diced
2 cups sliced mushrooms
½ cup pitted olives
½ cup chopped sun-dried tomatoes
1 large carrot, peeled and diced
2 cups zucchini, diced
½ cup wine or sherry
a handful of minced fresh herb (basil,
    dill, oregano, or parsley)

Serve sauce warm over pasta or in casseroles, etc. Or cool and freeze in plastic containers for easy meals ahead.

BBQ SAUCE

A tangy, tomato-based sauce for baking tofu, tempeh, or beans.

3 T. oil
1 large onion, diced
4 cloves garlic, minced
2 T. flour
1 T. chili powder
1 T. dijon mustard
dash of Worchestershire
dash of Tabasco
2 cups honey-sweetened ketchup
¼ cup molasses or barley malt
3 cups water (or 1 cup beer and
   2 cups water)
salt, pepper to taste

Heat oil in a 2 quart saucepan over medium heat. Sauté onion and garlic until lightly browned. Stir in flour; sauté until flour is browned, but not burnt. Add all other ingredients, stirring well. Bring to a boil. Reduce heat and simmer for one hour, uncovered, stirring occasionally. Sauce should thicken slightly as it cooks. Taste and adjust seasoning. If not for immediate use, allow the sauce to cool completely and refrigerate in a glass jar with a lid. Keeps for several weeks in the refrigerator.

SWEET AND SOUR SAUCE

*A tangy sweet glaze to accompany stirfried or steamed
vegetables, baked tofu, or tempeh.*

YIELD: 2 CUPS

2 T. oil
1 small onion, minced
3 cloves garlic, minced
1 small dried hot chili
1 T. grated fresh ginger
2 T. honey
2 T. tamari
4 T. rice or apple cider vinegar

In a 1 quart saucepan, heat oil
and sauté onion, garlic, chili,
and ginger. When onion is
lightly browned, add honey,
tamari, and vinegar. Heat until
bubbling. Discard chili.

⅔ cup orange juice
⅔ cup pineapple juice
1 T. cornstarch or arrowroot
    dissolved in a bowl with
        2 T. water

Whisk fruit juices into
saucepan. When heated
throughout, spoon 2 or 3 T. of
hot sauce into the bowl of
dissolved cornstarch. Slowly
whisk the warmed cornstarch
into the saucepan. Bring the
sauce to a low boil; cook to
desired consistency. Pineapple
chunks supply texture and a
lovely flavour; if desired. Add to
sauce at the end of cooking, and
heat throughout. Serve hot over
vegetables or tofu, with rice.

WALNUT SAUCE

*An elegantly simple Japanese relish for
baked tofu or stirfried green beans.*

SERVES 4

1½ cups walnut pieces
⅓ cup sake or mirin
¼ cup tamari

The walnut pieces should be
coarsely chopped (and, if you
wish, toasted). Mix with sake
and tamari in a small saucepan
and simmer for 3 to 5 minutes
over medium heat. Serve hot.
Spoon over slices of tamari-
baked tofu, or as a sauce over
cooked green beans, carrots, or
greens such as spinach.

TZATZIKI

This garlicky Greek sauce should be scooped up with crusty bread or raw vegetables. If you like garlic, it's addictive.

YIELD: 2 CUPS

2 to 3 cloves garlic
½ small English cucumber, diced
½ cup fresh mint or parsley leaves
1 t. salt
1 cup yogurt

In a blender or food processor, blend the garlic, mint, and cucumber in short, controlled bursts: they should be finely diced, but not liquified. Add salt and yogurt and blend very briefly to incorporate. Refrigerate and serve chilled.

Thicker (and thus more traditional) tzatziki can be made by draining the yogurt. Place the yogurt in a very fine mesh sieve (or wrap it in clean cheesecloth) and suspend over a cup. Leave the yogurt to drain for 1 to 2 hours, and then proceed with the recipe as written, discarding the drained liquid .

CREAMY SALAD DRESSING

This tasty salad dressing is swiftly assembled.

YIELD: 2 CUPS

1 cup lowfat yogurt
½ cup mayonnaise
3 T. lemon juice
1 clove garlic, minced
¼ cup minced green onions or chives
celery salt or herbed seasoning mix,
    to taste

With a fork or whisk, thoroughly blend all ingredients. Store refrigerated in an airtight container for up to 1 week. Shake before using.

HAVARTI CHEESE DIP

Creamy havarti cheese is blended with yogurt and just a hint of horseradish to make a sandwich spread or party dip for celery or crackers.

YIELD: 1 ½ CUPS

½ pound havarti, finely grated
½ cup yogurt
2 T. dijon mustard
1 to 2 t. horseradish (to taste)

Blend ingredients briefly in a food processor or blender, just until smooth.

4 green onions, diced
¼ cup fresh parsley, minced
salt, pepper to taste

Stir onions and parsley into cheese dip; season to taste. Chill. Best made 24 hours in advance, as the flavour improves overnight. Serve on crackers or bread, or as a dip with vegetables.

TOMATO CHUTNEY

This spicy relish makes the perfect condiment for Indian meals, or spooned over broiled tofu or tempeh. Store extra chutney in the refrigerator or freezer and dip into it often.

YIELD: 3 CUPS

8 to 10 medium tomatoes, peeled and chopped [or 1 (28 oz.) can tomatoes]
1 medium onion, finely diced
1" fresh ginger, peeled and grated
1 cup pitted, chopped dates
1 cup raisins
1 or 2 small hot peppers, seeded and minced (or hot oil or cayenne pepper to taste)
2 T. lemon or orange zest (optional)
1 t. salt

Stir all ingredients together in a heavy-bottomed saucepan. Bring to the boil, stirring. Reduce heat and simmer uncovered for about 2 hours, until chutney is thick. Stir occasionally to prevent sticking.

3 T. oil
3 T. mustard seeds

While the tomatoes are simmering, heat oil in a small pot with a lid. Add seeds: cover immediately. Fry the seeds on medium high heat until they stop popping. Add immediately to tomato sauce. Stir. Continue simmering until thick. Remove from heat and cool thoroughly. Store tightly sealed in a clean jar in the refrigerator. Keeps for 2 to 3 months.

CRANBERRY RELISH

*This recipe for the obligatory Thanksgiving relish offers the zest of citrus
fruits — just right to clear the palate during lavish Holiday meals.*

SERVES 6 TO 8

1 pound fresh cranberries
zest (peel) of 1 lemon
zest and juice of 1 lime
zest and fruit of 1 seedless orange
⅓ cup frozen orange juice
    concentrate
⅓ cup water
⅓ cup honey
¼ t. nutmeg
¼ t. allspice
¼ t. cinnamon
⅓ t. salt

Zest the citrus fruit. After zesting, peel the orange: discard all the white outer membrane, and chop the fruit. Add to half the cranberries, frozen concentrate, honey, and seasonings in a pot with a heavy bottom. Cook over medium low heat for 10 to 15 minutes. Stir often: this relish scorches easily. Add the remaining cranberries and cook for another 15 minutes. Sauce will thicken slightly when cool.

1 T. arrowroot or cornstarch
2 T. water

Dissolve arrowroot in water, and stir into the cranberries just before removing from heat. Stir thoroughly; then set aside to cool completely. Store in a sealed container in the refrigerator. This relish can be made in advance, and will keep for several weeks in the refrigerator or for 2 to 3 months in the freezer. Serve at room temperature.

Traditional for Holidays, this cranberry relish also goes nicely
with potato pancakes (Bram Bora'k, p. 144), or as a substitute
for chutney beside a curry dish.

MISO MAYONNAISE

An easy-to-make spread with an intriguing taste, and no cholesterol.
Handy on sandwiches or cabbage salads.

YIELD: 1 CUP

⅓ cup sweet white miso
¼ cup water
2 T. lemon juice
¼ to ½ t. mustard powder

Using a food processor or wire whisk, blend miso, water, and seasonings until smooth.

¼ to ⅓ cup sunflower oil

While whisking or blending, add the oil in a slow, steady trickle to the miso. Continue adding and whisking until mixture has the desired consistency. Adjust seasoning to taste. Store tightly sealed in the refrigerator for up to 2 weeks.

SALSA PICANTE

A spicy Tex-Mex tomato condiment that may be generously spooned over corn chips, chili, tacos, steamed vegetables, eggs, etc., or used in cooking. Adjust the heat to suit your taste.

3 T. oil
1, 2, or 3 small hot peppers, seeded and minced
1 large onion, diced
1 carrot, diced
5 cloves garlic, minced
1 red pepper, diced
1 green pepper, diced
1 T. oregano
1 T. cumin
1 T. ground coriander seeds
1 T. chili powder
1 T. vinegar

Heat oil in a skillet. Sauté vegetables and seasonings, covered, until tender. Process briefly in a blender or food processor until food is finely diced. Set aside to cool.

6 large tomatoes, chopped
juice of 3 limes
1 small bunch fresh cilantro, minced
½ cup fresh parsley, minced
salt, pepper to taste

Process the tomatoes, lime juice, and herbs in a blender or food processor until smooth. In a large bowl, mix the tomato sauce with the diced vegetables until thoroughly blended. Allow to cool thoroughly before refrigerating. Salsa keeps for about 2 weeks in an airtight jar. Freeze extra in plastic containers.

Seasonings:

Herbs, Spices & Condiments

Cooking without meat or with less butter or salt, you may find that you miss certain long-familiar flavours. This is where good seasoning makes such a difference: herbs, spices, and condiments will give a booster shot of flavour to your new diet.

There are several seasonings that I consider indispensable to life on this planet. Garlic, tamari, and nutritional yeast form a triumverate which helps to replace some of the rich flavour of meat. The rich dark taste of toasted sesame oil, the pungent bouquet of cilantro, a grind of fresh black pepper...these may be all it takes to translate a plate of steamed vegetables into a simple feast for the senses.

Many herbs and spices are classic features of more than one international cuisine. Keeping these in stock allows you to be versatile; with cumin, coriander, and chilis on hand, for example, you can cook Mexican chili and an Indian curry in the same week. Same seasonings, very different results. Fresh garlic packs a punch in most cuisines, whether it's called ajo or aille. Considered sacred in Central America, basil is also widely used in Indian and Thai cooking, and throughout the Mediterranean. Hot chilis add fiery interest from Jakarta to Santa Fe to Addis Abbaba.

Check the glossary for more information about herbs and spices: what they are, where they come from, how to use them.

The following tables give a quick overview of the predominant seasonings in several international cuisines. You'll see that a representative stock of herbs and spices permits you to move around the culinary world with ease, making your meals more interesting and extending the range of your cooking skills.

An example: if you've never previously cooked with cilantro (fresh coriander leaves) and wonder what you might do if you bought some...see p. 76, 89, and 124 for recipes from several traditions.

MAJOR SEASONINGS USED IN INTERNATIONAL CUISINES

(By no means a comprehensive list.)

ARGENTINIAN
Almonds
Basil
Bay leaf
Black pepper
Chilis
Nutmeg
Oregano
Turmeric
White pepper

CARIBBEAN
Allspice
Black pepper
Chilis
Coconut
Curries
Garlic
Lemon
Lime
Mango
Peanuts

CHINESE
Bean pastes
Chilis
Cilantro
Garlic
Ginger
Green onions
Hoisin sauce
Sczechuan pepper-
corns
Sesame oil
Soy sauce
Star anise

EASTERN EUROPEAN
Dill
Garlic
Marjoram
Onion
Paprika
Tarragon
Vinegar
Vodka

FRENCH
Capers
Cream
Dijon mustard
Dill
Garlic
Marjoram
Pepper
Shallots
Wine and spirits

GREEK
Bay leaf
Dill
Lemon
Mint
Olive oil
Oregano
Parsley
Rosemary

INDIAN
Bay leaf
Cardomom
Cinnamon
Chilis
Coriander
Cumin
Garlic
Ginger
Mustard seed
Saffron
Tamarind
Turmeric

INDONESIAN
Basil
Coconut meat
Coconut milk
Chilis
Garlic
Ginger
Lemon grass
Mint
Peanuts
Tamarind
Turmeric

ITALIAN
Basil
Bay leaf
Black pepper
Capers
Garlic
Olive oil
Oregano
Parsley
Rosemary
Sage
Tomatoes
Wine and spirits

JAPANESE
Ginger
Miso
Mirin
Rice vinegar
Seaweed
Tamari
Toasted sesame
Umeboshi plums
Wasabi

KOREAN
Ginger
Garlic
Hot chilis
Sesame oil and seeds
Soy pastes (called *changs*, like miso)
Soy sauce
Vinegar

MEXICAN
Achiote
Chilis (hot and mild, dried, roasted and fresh)
Cilantro
Cinnamon
Coriander
Cumin
Garlic
Lime
Onions
Oregano

MIDDLE EASTERN
Cayenne pepper
Cinnamon
Dried fruits
Garlic
Lemon
Mint
Olive oil
Parsley
Saffron
Tahini

MORROCAN
Caraway
Chilis
Cinnamon
Dried fruits
Garlic
Lemon
Mint
Saffron

SPANISH
Black pepper
Cinnamon
Cumin
Garlic
Olive oil
Paprika
Parsley
Pimento peppers
Saffron
Wine and spirits

THAI
Basil
Coriander
Galanga root
Garlic
Hot chilis
Kaffir limes
Lemon grass
Mint
Peanuts

VIETNAMESE
Basil
Chilis
Coriander
Garlic
Lemon grass
Lime
Mint
Peanuts

GUIDE TO HERBS, SPICES AND SEASONINGS

The history of seasonings around the world is a lesson in human migration, trade, exploration, and greed. Wars have been fought over spices; and some precious spices have been used as currency. The precise combination of specific seasonings is frequently a jealously guarded family secret, passed down for generations.

Spices are the dried seeds or berries of plants (nutmeg, coriander, and pepper are examples), ground or used whole to season a dish. *Herbs* are the leaves and stems of plants (basil, oregano, parsley, dill, etc.) used to impart delicate or pungent flavours to raw and cooked dishes. Learning to cook with spices and herbs is a delicious adventure. Experiment!

Dried herbs have more concentrated flavour than fresh herbs. When using fresh herbs, triple the quantity specified in dried form. Keep fresh herbs in the refrigerator. Store dried herbs in airtight containers in a cool spot out of direct sunlight. Purchase small quantities, so that they don't lose their flavour from waiting around.

ALLSPICE: a spice that borrows the flavours of other spices. Its name reflects the fact that allspice tastes a little of cinnamon and a little of nutmeg, with a hint of clove. Usually sold ground, allspice is the dried berry of a tree native to the Caribbean. Reliable for baking, excellent for seasoning vegetables such as squash and sweet potatoes. Makes a bright note in stews.

BASIL: an herb popular around the world for cooking, and in some cultures for religious purposes. Basil is probably best known for its pungent presence in Italian sauces, although it graces many other Mediterranean, Thai, and Indonesian dishes. Particularly good with tomatoes, lemon, garlic, oregano, and mint. Fresh leaves have more intense flavour, and a keener perfume, but dried basil works well in soups and sauces. Basil is the characteristic ingredient in **pesto**, a rich and distinctive paste of ground basil leaves. To make pesto: blend 2 cloves garlic, 1/2 cup parmesan cheese, 1/4 cup pine nuts, a dash of black pepper, and 3/4 cup (tightly packed) rinsed and drained fresh basil leaves in a blender or food processor until smooth. With the motor running, trickle in 1/3 cup good quality olive oil in a steady stream to form a thick paste. Toss with steaming, freshly drained pasta for a heady entrée; or spread on bread as an hors d'oeuvre. Use immediately, or store in a tightly-sealed jar; cover pesto with a thin layer of oil to prevent discolouration. Can be frozen in a plastic container for up to one month. This recipe will dress pasta for 4 people, with some left over.

BAY LEAF: also called laurel, from the tree whose shapely branches the Greeks twisted into wreathes for their heros. Dried bay leaves are used whole, contributing their subtle flavour to stock, slow-cooking soups, or sauces. The leaves should be removed and discarded when the dish is served. (Or you can choose to leave them…in my house we observe the tradition that the person whose serving includes the bay leaf is required to kiss the cook!)

BLACK PEPPER: Peppercorns are the dried berries of a tropical vine. Peppercorns provide a pungent aroma and a savoury hint of heat when ground. Black pepper is available ground or in whole corns, but as with most spices, its flavour is fresher and more potent if ground just before using. The peppercorn plant is not related to the family of chili or bell peppers.

CAPERS: the bud of a Mediterranean shrub that is pickled to provide a tangy seasoning in mayonnaises and sauces. Mince capers and combine them with lemon, garlic, and dill.

CARAWAY: A strongly-flavoured seed, familiar from rye or pumpernickel bread. Goes nicely with cabbage, and certain soups. A natural with dill and sour cream.

CARDOMOM: Sold as whole seed pods, or ground. Another aromatic spice with a distinctive flavour, cardomom is popular in such disparate cuisines as Indian, Scandinavian, and Arab. Enhances savoury dishes, such as curries, as well as coffeecakes and pastries.

CAYENNE: a red spice ground from very hot red peppers. Cayenne should always be added sparingly, a few potent grains at a time.

CHILIS: or peppers, as they are more commonly called, add interest to life – they range from the mild and sweet varieties to fireballs so lethal they provide tonsillectomies without benefit of surgery. You can't always predict from its appearance how hot any individual pepper will turn out to be, so proceed with caution (and a sense of adventure!).

Peppers are sold fresh, dried or canned. The mild peppers, generally called bell peppers, may be red, yellow, or green. Green varieties are called sweet peppers, poblanos, or Anaheims; the long thin yellow ones are known as banana peppers. All three colours may be used interchangeably, but red and yellow slivers make delightful visual accents. To prepare: remove seeds, stems, veins (the membranes inside the pepper that attach the seeds to the flesh), and cut out any blemishes; then chop, dice, julienne, or slice into thin rings.

Hot fresh chili peppers are usually smaller, from the thumb-sized jalapeños to the small green serranos, or the tiny curving red firebombs that are picturesquely known as "Devil's toenails." Equally hot are the beautiful red, yellow, and pale green peppers shaped like Chinese lanterns, called "Scotch bonnets" or Jamaican peppers. When selecting hot peppers, pick out firm, plump, unblemished ones. Handle with great caution. Carefully remove and discard the stem, veins, and seeds (the hottest part!). Mince the pepper very finely, then add raw or cooked to soups, stirfries, and dressings. Thoroughly wash your knife, cutting board, and hands. Whenever you handle fresh or dried hot peppers, be careful not to touch your face – eyes especially! – without first washing your hands. You may experience extreme discomfort – the feeling that your skin is on fire – if you rub your eyes or lips after cutting peppers. If you have sensitive skin, try wearing rubber gloves while working with the hot peppers.

Dried chilis are usually red and hot – you can buy them whole, crumbled, or powdered. To use whole dried chilis in dressings, soak 1 or 2 chilis in a few tablespoons of hot water for 5 minutes. Drain, reserving the liquid. Mince the chilis or put them through the blender with the reserved liquid; then add to a dressing or sauce. To flavour beans, simply drop one or two chilis in the pot when the beans begin to simmer. When beans are tender, remove and discard the chili pods.

To flavour cooking oil, heat oil and chili pod(s) together over medium-high heat for 3 to 5 minutes. Remove and discard the pod and any seeds. The flavoured oil adds zest to sautéed vegetables.

Canned chilis are available pickled or roasted, and range from mild to hot. Eat the pickled ones as condiments; dice the roasted chilis and add to beans, or bake into cornbread for a breath of the Southwest.

CHILI POWDER: this dried and powdered residue of a hot red pepper comes in a range of strengths, sometimes with other spices and seasonings added (notably sugar and salt in commercial mixes). Add chili powder cautiously, one tablespoon at a time, while sautéeing vegetables or simmering beans to achieve desired flavour and heat. Cooking chili powder thoroughly with the other ingredients will prevent the somewhat raw, bitter edge of the uncooked spice.

CILANTRO: a pretty herb that resembles flat leaf parsley, but can be distinguished by the pungent, slightly sweet aroma imparted by a crushed leaf. Sometimes called Chinese parsley, cilantro is actually the leaf portion of the coriander plant. Cilantro is a hallmark of Chinese, Mexican, and Indian cuisine. Its distinctive flavour tends to either be loved or hated. If you develop a taste for it, you will find that you are adding it to rice, hot sauces and relishes, salad dressings, and soups. Combines well with garlic, lemon, or lime juice.

CINNAMON: Ground or in stick form, cinnamon is one of the world's most widely used and beloved spices. Its familiar aroma and warm taste dominate sweets and desserts of all kinds, and underlie many curries. Break off an inch of cinnamon stick, and simmer it in Indian or Latin American soup.

COCONUT: Whole coconuts have a hard, fibrous shell encasing firm white flesh and a liquid called coconut water. This liquid is not to be confused with coconut milk, which is made by pulverizing fresh coconut meat into a thick pulp. Coconut milk can be purchased in cans for use in tropical soups, stews, and beverages. Coconuts characterize Caribbean, South American, Malaysian, and Thai cooking. High in fat, coconut should be used sparingly, as a treat.

CORIANDER: the seeds of the coriander plant (the leaf portion is called cilantro), ground to a powder and used in both Mexican and Indian cooking. Amenable with cumin, mustard seeds, anise, and fennel.

CUMIN: Cumin seeds are used extensively in Indian, Mexican and Middle Eastern kitchens. Whole or ground, cumin's warm savour is indispensable in curries or chili.

CURRIES: Curry refers to a combination of spices used in Indian cooking, or to a dish made with curry spices. There are as many curries as there are curry cooks; each family has its own favourite formulas for combining spices, taking into account both the ingredients and the occasion. Ranging from mild to hot, curries usually blend turmeric, coriander, cumin, fenugreek, cinnamon, cardomom, cayenne, or other spices. Freshly ground and blended curries are infinitely preferable to pre-packaged curry powder. Experiment to find your own favourite combinations for cooking curried vegetables, rice, tofu, or beans.

DILL: Delectable on pasta salads, potatoes, cucumbers. A perfect marriage with yogurt, dijon mustard, lemon, mint, or caraway.

GARLIC: Hard to imagine, a kitchen without this ubiquitous seasoning. Pungent raw garlic has a hot bite, leaves a lingering aroma. With slow and gentle cooking its flavour softens to an almost sweet, earthy mellowness. Fresh garlic is much more flavourful than when dried and granulated; see p. 196 for tips on processing your own ready-to-use garlic to store in the refrigerator.

GINGER: fresh ginger-root bears a pungent aroma and a bite, which mellows out when cooked. Its sharp, clean flavour forms an integral part of Chinese and other Asian cooking. Store the fresh root in an airtight container; do not refrigerate. To use, peel off the brown outer skin; grate with a fine grater, or slice into thin slices and then mince finely. Dried ginger will sometimes bring a bitter taste, so use fresh ginger whenever you can. Ginger brightens salad dressings, soups, and stirfries. A culinary pleasure with garlic, chilis, lemon grass, cilantro, and tamari.

LEMON: Lemon juice brightens dressings, soups, stirfries, and sauces. The perfect dressing for most steamed vegetables is a simple squeeze of fresh lemon juice. Grate (or thinly pare and mince) the zest of a lemon (the coloured portion of the peel: avoid the bitter white membrane) and sprinkle over salads, sauces, or coffeecakes. The volatile oils in the zest provide tangy notes of concentrated citrus flavour.

LEMON GRASS: a tropical grass with a distinctly lemon flavour, endemic in Indonesian and Thai cooking and a common ingredient in herbal teas. Heat the dried lemon grass in oil, then remove and discard. Use the flavoured oil for stirfrying.

LIME: The bright tang of lime juice makes a wonderful change of pace from lemon. A hallmark of Mexican, Indonesian, and Asian cooking, lime especially complements garlic, cilantro, tamari, chilis, and cumin. A highlight for salad dressings, steamed vegetables, stews, or iced beverages.

MARJORAM: an aromatic herb similar to oregano, although not quite as strongly flavoured. Drop in any recipe calling for a nice "herby" taste that isn't overbearing; useful in soups, sauces, omelettes. Goes well with parsley and basil.

MINT: peppermint and spearmint leaves lend their cool, clean presence to many Asian, Mediterranean, and Indian specialties, from curries to tabouli. Keep a pot of mint in your kitchen window to freshen iced teas, and wake up salads. Fresh mint leaves are a graceful garnish for savoury dishes as well as fruit salads and desserts. Dried mint can be substituted in cooking, but the essence of the herb is considerably diminished in dried form.

MIRIN: a Japanese rice wine, for cooking, that is clear, sweet and potent. Use sparingly to add a touch of sweetness to soups and sauces or to counteract the impact of other sour and salty tastes in cooking.

MISO: a salty Japanese paste that is low in fat, high in protein and vitamin B12, and packed with flavour. It is made by cooking, aging and fermenting soybeans, which are then sometimes mixed with other grains to make different flavours of miso such as genmai (brown rice), mugi (barley), or lighter, sweeter shiro (white rice). Misos vary in flavour and in colour from white to red to dark brown, with many shades in between. The darker misos have been fermented for a longer period, and are stronger and saltier in flavour. Miso may be stored indefinitely at room temperature. An excellent soup base when dissolved in hot water, miso should not be boiled; boiling destroys its nutritional properties.

MUSTARD: the seeds of the mustard plant are available in three forms. *Whole seeds* are found in Indian cooking, usually fried in hot oil until they pop, adding their distinctive taste and texture to curries. The seeds are also ground into *powder*, ready to be made into prepared mustard or to use sparingly in cooking to flavour sauces. *Prepared mustard* is a condiment of mustard powder dissolved in liquid (wine, water or vinegar). Many cuisines produce a variety of prepared mustard, from France's classic Dijon, to Germany's tangy brown spread, to China's hot relish for dipping.

NUTRITIONAL YEAST: not to be confused with baking yeast or brewer's yeast, nutritional yeast is a condiment, added to casseroles, salads, toast, popcorn, and drinks for its nutritional value and cheese-like flavour. Nutritional yeast, a pure yeast culture which is grown, fermented, pasteurized, and dried, is high in B vitamins and protein. Similar to Engevita yeast and sometimes called good-tasting yeast, it can be stored indefinitely in an airtight container.

NUTMEG: the nutmeg, about the size of a pecan, is the solid, hard nut of a tropical tree. Although available ground, it's well worth the effort to grate your own powder. Scrape the nut against the smallest holes on your grater, or look for a special nutmeg grater, with tiny holes. Sprinkle the aromatic dust over stirfries, curries, and baked goods. Superb with spinach.

OLIVE OIL: the joy of the Mediterranean and the Middle East for centuries by virtue of its rich, fruity flavour, olive oil turns out to be beneficial, as a mono-unsaturated fatty acid, in lowering cholesterol. Olive oil is sold in several grades (and at corresponding prices) that indicate the number of pressings. Find one whose bouquet you enjoy, and drizzle sparingly over salads. Obligatory in Italian sauces, and for sautéeing many vegetables.

OREGANO: frequently partnered with basil, oregano is an herb of Mediterranean origin. The Greeks grill with oregano and sprinkle it over salad; Italians lean heavily upon oregano for tomato sauce. Perfect in vegetable sautées, soups, and stews; with garlic, rosemary, lemon, parsley, or mint.

PAPRIKA: a red pepper, dried and powdered. Dust paprika over potato salads or casseroles for colour; sauté with onions for flavour. A note of caution: paprika burns easily, so reduce the heat when cooking and stir often to prevent scorching. Paprika is available in two varieties: hot Hungarian, and mild, sweet Spanish. Check the label before shaking generously.

PARSLEY: indispensable to European, North American, and Middle Eastern cuisine. Curly-leaf parsley is used as a garnish and in cooking. Flat-leaf parsley, also called Italian parsley, has more flavour. Dried parsley makes a poor substitute for the rich colour and savour of minced fresh parsley, added in the final minutes to stews or soups, or when sautéeing vegetables. Parsley goes well with garlic, lemon, onion, and almost any other herb.

ROSEMARY: the fragrant leaves of an evergreen shrub. Rosemary is the traditional symbol for remembrance and a standard item in the European traditon of cooking with fresh herbs. The needle-like leaves are pungent and should be used sparingly. As with other herbs, the flavour of fresh rosemary is most delightful; if you use dried herb, coarsely grind the dried leaves just before cooking.

SAFFRON: rare, costly, delicate, and gorgeous in hue, saffron is actually the stigma of a flower. A tiny pinch imparts the rich reddish colour and distinctive flavour of this ancient herb. Turmeric makes a workable, less expensive, (though less wonderful) substitute.

SAGE: germane to Mediterranean and American cuisine, sage is a particularly pungent member of the mint family. Natives of the American Southwest burned sage leaves for purification. Fresh sage brings the sharpest flavour, but if not available, rubbed dried leaves are superior to the ground powder. Sage goes well with garlic, onion, lemon, and thyme. Use sparingly.

SESAME: the rich, satisfying flavour of sesame is available via several routes. The *seeds* can be added to baked goods, or stirred into sauces. Natural foods stores sell seeds with the hull (which contains most of the nutrition) still attached; these should be cracked slightly for easier digestion. The seeds are commonly ground into a nut butter called *tahini*, a staple ingredient of Middle Eastern sauces and dressings. You can use tahini as a thickener in gravy or as a sandwich filling. *Sesame oil* is a light, flavourful oil for stirfries. Don't confuse it with the *oil from toasted sesame seeds*, manufactured in Japan. The latter rich, aromatic, dark brown oil is a heady condiment rather than a cooking oil. Use it sparingly to season stirfries and dressings. Also from Japan come the black sesame seeds which add a delightful visual accent.

SOY SAUCE: a dark, intensely salty condiment from Asian cooking, soy sauce is a byproduct of soybeans. See TAMARI.

TABASCO: the familiar brand name for a hot pepper sauce, made from peppers and vinegar. It provides concentrated heat – add a few drops at a time to chili or salad dressing. Tabasco-style pepper sauce should not be confused with tomato-based spicy condiments, sometimes called picante sauce or salsa (see p. 208 for a salsa recipe).

TAMARI: Japanese soy sauce, usually made without wheat or the additives and colouring agents found in many commercial soy sauces. An indispensable flavouring, tamari gives rich salty taste and dark brown colour to soups, sauces, marinades, or vegetables, and can be used as a lower-sodium replacement for salt at the table. Shoyu is similar to tamari, but may contain wheat. Check the label, as the two names are sometimes used interchangeably here in the West. Please do not be tempted to use the commercial brands that have long been available here, as the sweeteners and other additives produce a greatly inferior flavour.

TAMARIND: a tropical fruit with a rich sweet/sour taste, featured in Malaysian, West Indian, and Indian dishes. Indian or Asian groceries sell jars of tamarind paste, a dark, dense concentrate of cooked fruit. Spoon a dollop into split pea soup, or make a chutney-style sauce to use over vegetables and rice.

TURMERIC: a deep, yellow-orange powder, turmeric is one of the spices commonly used in curry. It can be a little bitter until it is cooked. It goes well with onions, garlic, mustard seeds and cumin. Use it to add a rich yellow colour to rice, pilafs, soups, potatoes, or egg salads.

UMEBOSHI PLUM PASTE: a rosy paste of Japanese plums that have been pickled in salt with beefsteak leaves. Intensely sour and salty, small quantities may be stirred into soups and dressings to enhance flavour. Umeboshi paste is also believed to have medicinal properties, helpful in relieving acid indigestion and some headaches.

VINEGARS: a tart, acidic liquid used around the world as a condiment and as a preservative for pickling. Vinegars are byproducts of the fermenting process, and are commonly made from apple cider, rice, or wine. Sometimes they are flavoured with herbs or spices. Besides adding tartness and flavour to many recipes, vinegar also aids digestion. To make a vinaigrette dressing for salads or vegetables, blend two parts oil to one part vinegar; whisk with herbs of your choice to make your own herbed vinegars.

I recommend that you use refined white vinegar for cleaning purposes only (Newspapers dipped in vinegar make an excellent nontoxic, nonstreaking glass cleaner; and vinegar acts as a grease-cutter in dishwashing).

WORCHESTERSHIRE SAUCE: a tangy, dark brown condiment made from vinegar, tamarind and spices. Sprinkle a few drops at a time into vegetarian chili, or add to a tofu marinade or black-eyed peas. (Please note: Worchestershire sauce does contain a small amount of anchovy concentrate. If you are avoiding fish altogether, omit Worchestershire from the recipe.)

HOW TO MAKE A VEGETARIAN DIET EASY – PLANNING AHEAD & CONVENIENCE FOODS

These days convenience foods are a way of life for most people. What about vegetarians? This chapter outlines time-saving techniques for integrating vegetarian meals into a crowded lifestyle, and advice on making and purchasing vegetarian convenience foods.

1) Plan ahead. Put the rice or beans on to cook for tomorrow's dinner while you're cooking tonight's; 5 to 10 minutes of prep time, and then it's pretty well effortless. While you're eating and cleaning up after today's meal, the basis of tomorrow's dinner is cooking itself. Be sure the rice or beans have thoroughly cooled before you cover them and store them in the fridge.

One good way to reheat rice: place it in the basket of a steamer (the flat bamboo style holds more and heats more evenly) and steam for several minutes, until heated throughout. Alternatively, place the rice in an ovenproof casserole, sprinkle with a few drops of water, cover, and heat in the oven.

Cooked beans should be returned to the boil for 3 minutes, then simmered, stirring, until heated throughout.

2) Plan your meals to take advantage of these precooked staples. If you're serving stirfried vegetables over rice, cook enough to have 2 cups of cooked rice left over for tomorrow's Andalusian Cream of Tomato Soup (p.59). Or if you cook a pot of chickpeas, cook more than you need: freeze the extra peas in their cooking liquid, in small portions in plastic containers. Pull out and thaw; you've got the base for hummus or minestrone soup, or to toss into a salad, or to dress up in Mexican Greens with Potatoes and Garbanzos (p.145).

Always cook enough beans of any variety to yield an extra few cups of cooked beans. Extra cooked beans can be added to soups and stews to give body and protein. Some recipes where cooked beans would prove handy: Texas Taco Salad (p. 158), Vegetable Chowder (p. 62), Nachos (p. 155), or Stew à la Tarragon (p. 119). Beans will keep for several days in the fridge. But they can go bad after that, so if you don't plan to use them within 3 days of cooking, freeze beans in their cooking liquid after cooling. They'll last for several weeks in the freezer.

3) Check your basement to see if you still have a "crockpot". If you don't, consider investing in one of these slowcookers, which will cook dried beans overnight or while you're at work. They're also superb for keeping apple cider or chili steaming hot when you have a crowd over for hockey or Girl Guides or those endless political meetings.

4) Buy canned beans if you really feel that you just don't have the time or energy to cook your own. Do look for brands that don't contain meat byproducts, or chemical additives, and do be aware of the salt content of canned foods before adding extra salt to the recipe.

5) Explore the grains that don't take so long to cook. Bulghar and couscous are both swiftly prepared. Quinoa and millet take only 20 to 25 minutes to cook, which is hardly longer than white rice. All of these go well with stirfries and stews or as an accompaniment to vegetable dishes. Cornmeal simmers in about 25 minutes into a thick porridge called polenta, frequently served in Italy and Eastern Europe.

CONVENIENCE FOODS

An endless variety of products in the mainstream market are designed to save you time: instant mixes in pouches, pre-made sauces in jars, whole frozen dinners that can be heated in minutes. Unfortunately, these products come laden with artificial flavours, colouring agents, and preservatives. And they are often meant to be used on or with meat. If you're in the habit of using convenience foods, but you'd like to eat vegetarian meals, you have three options. First, realize that a well-stocked spice cabinet and a little experience with seasonings will quickly make the prepackaged mixes redundant. Second, natural foods stores now carry a growing selection of convenience foods for vegetarians, some of them high-quality with healthier ingredients. Third, and best: you can learn to make vegetarian convenience foods at home.

Visit your local natural foods store to see what's available. In the freezer case, you'll find enticing entrées, tortillas, prepared vegetable casseroles, and desserts, including nondairy substitutes for ice cream. On the shelves you'll discover boxed mixes for pilafs, whole grain pancake mixes, just-add-water falafel mix, quick-cooking cereals. There are bottled salad dressings and sauces and canned soups. These products are usually made without as much salt or added sugar as their mainstream equivalents, and are often available with organic ingredients (But again: read labels!). Vegetarian convenience foods may not taste exactly like the products you grew up with. But remember that often what tastes familiar is the taste of salt, sugar, and MSG. When you make the move to a vegetarian diet, you take your tastebuds with you, and part of the challenge is educating your taste buds to appreciate less adulterated ingredients. Again, sometimes the prices will be higher than for the less healthy equivalents. You'll have to choose, whether the higher quality of the food justifies paying for convenience.

Among your other convenience food options are the meat substitutes. These non-meat entrées include tofu hot dogs (sometimes referred to as *not dogs*), tempeh and tofu burgers, and bacon and sausage substitutes. Different brands taste differently, so experiment to find out which ones appeal the most to you. Do remember that these products are not made from meat, and will not taste the same as a hot dog or burger, even if that's what they resemble. But they may prove useful as you make the transition to meatless meals, or if your vegetarian kids want to be included in cooking over a campfire.

Freezing your own home-cooked foods can be an easy, inexpensive way to stock "instant" meals. Many of the recipes in this book freeze well. Cool food quickly to room temperature before sealing in airtight plastic containers; place in the freezer. (You're making your own life easier if you freeze food in portions suitable to the size of your family.) Label and date each container with masking or freezer tape. Thaw overnight in the refrigerator, at room temperature for 2 to 3 hours, or in a bath of warm water for a few minutes. Soups, stews, and casseroles are excellent examples of foods that lend well to freezing. It's not much more work to increase or double a recipe, cook more than you need at the moment, and freeze the extra for future use on those nights when you won't have the time to cook.

SHOPPING FOR A VEGETARIAN DIET

So where do I buy all these new ingredients? you ask.

No problem! In the first place, many of the components of your vegetarian diet are already waiting in your cupboard — pasta, rice, beans, potatoes — and your refrigerator — eggs, cheese, fresh fruits, and vegetables. Your local grocery store is an excellent place to stock your kitchen for meatless meals.

In response to the new consciousness about health and diet, more and more grocery stores now carry tofu and other "health food" products. But you may have to go further afield for several of the ingredients cited in this book: to a natural foods store, or an Oriental market if there's one in your neighbourhood. If you think that a trip to a natural foods store will be a perilous excursion into alien territory, think again. The people who work in natural food stores tend to be very interested in health and diet. I think you'll generally find that these people are friendly, knowledgeable, and ready to be helpful with any questions you have about products you don't recognize, or techniques for using those products. Indeed, for many people, the friendly atmosphere and sense of community that they find at their local natural foods store makes shopping a treat to be anticipated, rather than a chore to be endured.

The most important trick to shopping, wherever you do it, is READING. Read labels. Look for brands with the least processing, the fewest additives and preservatives, no added salt or sugar. Keep in mind that you and your family will consume everything listed on that label. Become aware of what you eat, and consciously choose what will go into your body.

Two truths to remember while you're shopping:

1) YOU ARE WHAT YOU EAT.

2) GOOD INGREDIENTS MAKE GOOD FOOD.

Obviously the ideal diet would comprise whole grains, dried beans, and fresh produce, organically grown to avoid pesticides. But this may not be possible: such products may not be available where you live, and the time you have for meal preparation may be limited. So make what changes you can, when you can. It will probably be easier to accomplish a series of small changes in your diet over a period of time – unless you are one of those people who chooses to go cold turkey (or should we say cold tofu?) on bad eating habits. The goal, however you make it happen, is to replace overprocessed, oversweetened, high-cholesterol food with fresh vegetables, beans, and grains which are loaded with nutrition rather than additives. Here are some suggestions for stocking your vegetarian kitchen.

When shopping at your local grocery store, pick up:
Canned tomatoes (whole and crushed)
Frozen peas and corn
Pasta in several shapes and sizes
Potatoes
Onions
Garlic
Carrots
Canned beans (kidney, pinto, chick peas, black-eyed peas,
    lentils) for emergencies
Honey
Lowfat milk and yogurt, cottage cheese, ricotta, and other
    cheeses (try to avoid coloured cheeses which contain dyes)

When shopping at your natural foods store, look for:
Produce: you may wish to purchase fruits and vegetables where you can obtain organic produce. It's sometimes more expensive, but it may be worth the extra expense to avoid the chemical pesticides on non-organic produce. And if enough people buy organic produce, the prices will come down as more farmers grow organic to meet the demand.
Bulk Items: While a little less convenient than pre-packaged food, bulk shopping is cheaper and lets you decide how much you buy of any item. Experiment with a trial quantity of couscous or cumin seeds, for example, rather than buying what might turn out to be a lifetime supply.

The following items can be purchased in bulk:
Raisins and other dried fruit
Organic white and whole wheat flour
Oats
Rice
Dried beans
Spices and dried herbs – buy small amounts of several different
   kinds. Remember to label the unfamiliar ones at the store, so
   that once you get home you'll have some idea what you bought.
Nuts
Couscous
Bulghar wheat
Granola
Popcorn – a healthy snack food
Nut butters (peanut, almond, hazelnut, cashew butters, etc.)

Other basics:
Good quality oils (sunflower or canola, sesame, toasted sesame,
   peanut, corn, olive, walnut)
Free-range eggs
Tamari or Shoyu (good quality soy sauce)
Tofu (often also available at your local grocery store in the dairy or
   produce section)
Tempeh (in the freezer section)
Breads and crackers

Healthy convenience foods:
Vegetarian soup bases, frozen entrées, tofu burgers or hot dogs,
   breakfast cereals, dried mixes

Before heading out to the grocery store, read through the
sections in this book on staples, convenience foods, and seasonings, and leaf through the recipes. Pick one or two recipes with
unfamiliar ingredients. Why not take this book with you on your
first few trips to the natural foods store? You'll be able to look up
any items you're not sure how to use, and to check that you have
all the ingredients for any recipes that you decide to try.

And while you're moving in the right direction – making
food choices because of their impact on your internal environment

– keep in mind the external environment. You make a big difference when you change your consumption habits. Choose products with **a minimum of excess packaging**. Choose products that come in **recyclable containers** instead of disposable. Tell the store owner or manager that you prefer to buy environmentally-friendly products, and encourage her or him to carry a wide range of products that are minimally packaged, free from chemical additives, and not harmful to the earth. Shop with your own cloth or string shopping bags, or bring back and reuse the store's plastic bags.

Take a look under your kitchen sink. How many of your cleaning supplies are marked with the symbol for poison? How many warn you to avoid contact with this product, to avoid breathing it in, or spilling it on your skin? Consider that the earth is a closed-cycle environment, and that what goes down the drain or into the garbage or up into the ozone, must come back to us in the food we eat, the water we drink, and the air we breathe. Maybe it's time to switch to less harmful cleansers, baking soda for scrubbing, and vinegar to cut grease. Your local environmental organization will have further information on safe cleansers; there's also a bibliography at the back of this book.

These may seem small steps, or even major hassles. But each habit of consumption that you change from thoughtless to conscious, from harmful to healthy, is another step on the road to a saner, more balanced, healthier life, for you and for the planet…and another way to feel good about yourself.

KITCHEN EQUIPMENT

All of us have our favourite kitchen tools, usually based on the traditions within which we grew up. An irreplaceable tool to one cook may be only a useless gadget to another. Not that you need to buy a lot of specialized tools to be a vegetarian cook. But there are some basic kitchen tools that make life easier for the vegetarian cook.

I have a friend who compares cooking to computers: think of cookbooks as the software, and pots, knives, and utensils as the hardware. Your output is only as efficient as your software and hardware allow. Here's the list of hardware I'd recommend.

KNIVES:
- one chef's knife, with an 8" stainless or carbon steel blade;
- one or two good quality paring knives (2 to 3" blades)
- one small knife with a 3 to 4" serrated blade (for tomatoes, etc.)
- one knife with an 8 to 10" serrated blade, for slicing bread

I consider good quality knives, kept sharp, to be the most fundamental and necessary tools of a cook. Face it: you'll be cutting up a lot of vegetables when you prepare vegetarian meals. Your work can be made both safer and simpler if you use sharp, sturdy knives.

Good quality knives are well-balanced, feel stable in your grip, are of a length that is easy for you to work with, and will maintain a sharp edge. They can be expensive, but with proper care they'll last a lifetime. Knives should be treated with respect, as you would treat any other high-quality tool. Do not use them as blunt instruments, hammers or crowbars. Knives should be washed immediately after use, dried and stored in a rack. Have them professionally sharpened periodically, or learn how to sharpen them properly yourself. Purchase a steel (the sword-shaped sharpening tool); use it daily to maintain that sharp edge on your knives.

A chef's knife tapers to a point at its tip, the blade forming an elongated triangle. Cutting is fast and easy once you've learned to keep the tip of the blade in contact with the cutting surface, push the food to be cut under the knife with one hand while raising the handle up and down rapidly with the other. Keep the tips of your fingers safely out from under the blade as it comes down. With practice, this technique will considerably shorten your preparation time.

Please use your common sense with knives. Don't frustrate yourself by trying to mince parsley or garlic with a paring knife; a big chef's knife works better. Conversely, don't try to peel an apple with a long knife; that's why a paring knife was invented. Never cut toward your hand or body, always push the knife blade away. Pay attention when using sharp knives, cuts always happen when you get drawn into conversation or otherwise distracted. Never leave knives lying near the edges of counters to be knocked or pulled off onto feet or short people. And never leave them floating in a cloud of murky dishwater or under a pile of dishes. Knives work best when they're sharp; use them safely and they'll increase your pleasure in cooking.

POTS AND PANS:

- 1 quart, 2 quart and 4 quart stainless steel pots, well balanced, with lids and heat resistant handles. Thick bottoms spread out the heat evenly and help prevent scorching.
- one Dutch oven or other ovenproof casserole pan with lid, stainless steel, enamelware or ceramic.
- 9" skillet (cast-iron or nonstick)
- baking sheet with a rim (stainless steel or nonstick)
- wok with a lid and a long handle
- small saucepan for melting butter, etc. (stainless steel)
- baking pans: a 9 x 13" casserole pan (glass or ceramic)
  an 8" square pan
  loaf or muffin pans

I recommend stainless steel over aluminum because of the recent research suggesting a connection between Alzheimer's disease and high levels of aluminum in the human body. Trace amounts of aluminum can apparently leach out of aluminum cookware into the food that we cook. Stainless steel is sturdy and long-lasting, and it will not take on odors or colours from food. Inexpensive, thin pots may be cheaper in the short run, but over the long run they'll cause aggravation and ruin food by scorching. It's my experience that high-quality pots with extra-thick bottom surfaces, designed to be well-balanced, are a worthwhile investment.

Woks and cast-iron skillets work best when they're seasoned. This means that a coat of oil has been cooked into the surface of the pan to ensure smooth, even cooking without scorching or sticking. When a wok or skillet is new, or when it has lost its seasoning through mishandling, it can be reseasoned. Coat the cooking surface with a light, even layer of sunflower oil (or another flavourless oil). Use a paper towel to wipe out the excess. Over a low burner or in a low oven, gently heat the skillet or wok for 30 minutes to an hour until the oil is absorbed (think of it as slowly baking the oil into the surface of the pan until it forms a seal). If you treat the pan with care, seasoning will only rarely be necessary.

To care for a pan once it has been seasoned, do not soak it in water, and do not use soap on it. As soon as you've finished cooking, give the pan a quick scrub with a plastic scourer, and rinse it well. Set on a low burner or in the oven to dry, and once it is dry put it away immediately to keep it from rusting. Don't dry it with a towel (gets the towel black and the pan covered with lint). And try not to burn food in the pan (bad for the pan and for the food).

KITCHENWARE & UTENSILS:
- set of 3 or 4 mixing bowls, assorted sizes (glass, ceramic, stainless steel or plastic)
- vegetable steamer (the folding metal variety that fits inside pots, or the basket-type bamboo or metal steamer with a lid that sits on top of pots)
- colander/strainer for draining pastas, rinsing beans, etc. (metal or plastic)
- grater – preferably a sturdy, multi-sided metal grater with a variety of sharp holes to shred or grate cheese, vegetables, orange peel, etc.
- vegetable peeler – sturdy, and one that actually works (some peelers are so dull that using them is like trying to whittle with a butter knife)
- whisk – medium-size, with a comfortable handle
- rubber spatulas for scraping out bowls and jars
- small metal strainer with a handle for straining vegetable broth

APPLIANCES:
- food processor – I suppose these ubiquitous electric appliances, branded with the yuppie stigma, are the ultimate gadget. I know cooks got along fine for thousands of years without them, but then people who did the cooking, usually women and mothers, used to spend most of their days preparing food. Today food processors take the place of graters, knives, whisks, mortar and pestle and a lot of elbow grease. It's up to you to decide if you'll use one often enough to justify the expense, and if the hassle of pulling it out, setting it up and then washing all the parts is worth the work they save. Sometimes I think they're more bother than they're worth, but not when I'm using mine to grate potatoes for potato pancakes, or to make hummus, or to finely chop nuts, or to mince 3 heads of garlic, or to make perfectly blended salad dressing.
- blender – doesn't perform as many tasks as a food processor, but it's very handy for making creamy soups, salad dressings, and

fruit shakes
- electric coffee grinder and spice mill – another luxury item, but if you grind spices like coriander or fennel just before cooking a curry, the flavour will be much fresher and more intense. The same work can be done by a mortar and pestle, but the electric grinder is much faster.

GADGETS:

Some people are genetically programmed to be unable to resist gadgets. I'm one of them; when a new gadget is invented, I immediately feel that I cannot live without it. Even if I don't know what it does. In saner moments, I will acknowlege that I seldom, if ever, use some of the gadgets that have called out my name in kitchenware stores. Nonetheless, gadgets follow me home and line the drawers of my kitchen: egg slicers, olive pitters, decorating tools, mushroom brushes, salad spinners.

It's perfectly possible to be a good cook and to produce fine meals without having your own personal citrus zester, a handy little gizmo that carves fine strips of peel from oranges and lemons. And if you are one of those people who can turn your back on such a wonderful tool, then good for you. I personally own two zesters, one for home and one to take on catering jobs. When I fall for a gadget, I fall hard.

You decide whether you can live without the following:
- salad spinner
- olive pitter (hinged handles that meet in a metal ring to hold the olive in place, and a merciless prong for pushing out the pit; does a nice job on fresh cherries, too)
- melon ballers (a small, rounded scoop for shaping fruit into clean, symmetrical spheres)
- nutmeg grater (small-sized grater with tiny holes to scrape whole nutmegs into into an intensely flavourful powder)
- ginger grater – small ceramic dish with lots of sharp prongs to scrape/grate fresh gingerroot, instead of mincing
- tea ball – immersed in soups or other boiling liquids so that the essence of whole spices, such as clove or dried chili, can soak out through the pores of the tea ball; the ball is then readily removed and the spices easily discarded

A GLOSSARY OF INGREDIENTS
& KITCHEN TERMS

AL DENTE: an Italian phrase meaning "to the tooth." Pasta that is *al dente* has been cooked until it is firm – neither raw in the middle nor mushy. Different kinds and shapes of noodles require different cooking times, so you'll have to use your own judgement, and your own "dentes." Fresh pasta can be counted on to cook in about a third of the time that dried pasta requires. See *Shocking* for cooking technique.

ARROWROOT: arrowroot flour is a bland, thickening starch obtained from a tropical plant, an easy substitute for corn starch. Mix with a little water or cooking liquid to make a smooth paste before adding it to hot liquids. Stir the paste gradually into soup or sauce. Do not overcook once thickened.

BLANCHING: a method of boiling vegetables very briefly. Place at least twice the quantity of water to vegetables in a pot large enough to hold both water and vegetables with room left over. Bring the water to a rolling boil. Leaving the heat on high, add washed and sliced vegetables for 60 to 120 seconds. (I'm not kidding, don't get distracted and wander off.) Strain or drain off the boiling water; place the vegetables immediately in a bowl of very cold water to cover. This will stop the cooking process, and prevent the vegetables from turning to mush. Blanching brightens the colour of vegetables while leaving them fairly crisp and not really cooked – not too far from raw, but more welcoming to the tooth. Blanching also allows for easy peeling of tomatoes and some fruits (peaches, etc.).

DAIKON RADISH: a large white radish with a bit of a bite when eaten raw, but a slightly sweet taste when cooked. Peel fresh daikon and grate over salads, or dice or julienne to cook in stirfries or soups. Dried shredded daikon is available in packages. Rehydrate by boiling for 20 to 30 minutes and then leaving to soak for 2 to 3 hours. Drain and use as fresh.

DICE: to cut up vegetables in even, consistent pieces, each the size of the tip of your index finger. (Although that is where any connection between dicing and the ends of your fingers should come to a screeching halt.)

FINELY DICE: to cut up vegetables in even, consistent pieces the size of a kernel of corn.

EMULSIFY: to mix oils and other liquids together in such a way that they form a stable, thicker blend that will not separate into its component parts. To emulsify a salad dressing, mix together the seasonings with water, lemon juice, or vinegar as desired. Then while whisking vigorously or blending in the food processor, slowly trickle in a steady stream of oil.

GUMBO: an African word, originally another name for okra. But in Louisiana, gumbo has come to mean a variety of thick stews (Okra Gumbo, p. 120). You may have heard of filé gumbo; filé is sassafras leaves ground and used as flavouring and a natural thickener in gumbo.

Gumbo is the probably the best known example of Cajun cooking. Cajuns are the descendents of French colonials from Atlantic Canada, forced to resettle in Louisisana in the early 1700's; and their cuisine reflects the marriage of French cooking with a new set of ingredients.

HONEY: a sweetener produced by bees, honey derives its distinctive flavour from the flowers which supplied the bees with nectar. Buckwheat honey, for instance, is more strongly flavoured than clover or orange blossom honey. Try several varieties to find your own favourite. Honey is more intensely sweet than white sugar, so reduce the amount used when substituting by about half. The substitution of honey for white sugar will also affect the texture of baked goods to varying degrees.

JICAMA: This delicious and versatile root vegetable is grown in Mexico. Peel away the pale brown leathery skin to uncover a crisp, moist, slightly sweet tuber with a taste and texture somewhere between apple and celery. Grate it for salads, or slice and eat raw for a cool treat. Jicama keeps its crisp texture when cubed and simmered for use in stews and soups.

JULIENNE: to cut vegetables in slender, even, consistent pieces the size and shape of wooden matches, or slightly larger.

KNEAD: to work dough or pastry by hand until it is thoroughly mixed, elastic and smooth. Fold dough over on itself and push edges to the centre with the heel of the hand, while turning the dough in a circle. How the dough is kneaded will affect the consistency and texture of the finished product (but be careful: more is NOT always better when it comes to kneading pastry).

KOMBU: a mineral-rich seaweed with broad flat fronds. Drop a small (3 to 6") strip into a pot of beans while cooking, to enhance flavour and make the beans more digestible. Discard when the beans are cooked.

MAPLE SYRUP: a golden sweet syrup processed from the sap of maple trees. This rich, delicious sweetener may seem a luxury item, but the high cost begins to make sense when you learn that it takes 40 gallons of sap (the yield of one good-sized tree in a good year) boiled down to make one gallon of maple syrup. Maple syrup is sold in grades; grade A is more refined and lighter in colour, grade C darker and richer in minerals. Maple syrup is potent, so use relatively small amounts to establish that distinctive and luxurious flavour.

MINCE: to cut (fresh herbs or garlic, for instance) with a sharp knife so finely that the pieces are as small as the head of a pin. Garlic may be pressed through a garlic press, minced with a knife, or processed in a food processor.

OILS: a large variety of cholesterol-free vegetable oils are available: these contain mono-unsaturated or polyunsaturated fatty acids, which help the body to reduce cholesterol levels. But it's also important to limit our overall intake of fats. Doctors recommend that no more than 30% of our daily calorie intake come from fats. Oils are fats, so use them sparingly. Bake with lighter oils, such as sunflower or soy. Experiment with different varieties such as olive, walnut, or sesame for their distinct flavour in cooking or in dressings. Look for the less refined, cold-pressed brands packaged in glass containers, and store oils in the refrigerator to prevent them from going rancid.

OKRA: a green vegetable also known as ladyfingers because of its shape. Found in dishes in Africa, Greece, India, China, and the American South, okra may be boiled, pickled, curried, stirfried, or breaded and fried. Frying it, or combining it with tomatoes helps to cut okra's viscosity. Select okra that is relatively small, crisp and unblemished; avoid large or flaccid (tough) specimens. Trim and discard both ends, rinse and drain well. See the recipe for Okra Gumbo, p. 120.

PEPPERS: see *Chilis* .

PICANTE SAUCE: "Picante" is Spanish for hot, or highly-seasoned. Picante sauce is a spicy and flavourful tomato-based sauce with diced vegetables, garlic, chilis, and other seasonings. And it's practically a way of life throughout the Southwest and Mexico, where it's used as a topping for chips, tacos, nachos, steamed vegetables, and scrambled eggs. Don't be tempted to omit this ingredient – find a brand that you enjoy or make your own and use it liberally. There are several good commercial brands available. To make your own, see p. 208. Picante sauce is sometimes called salsa, a name that is loaned to a Mexican dance that also puts fire in your veins.

PINE NUTS: also called pignolas or piñons, pine nuts are harvested from pine cones, and characterize both Mediterranean and Southwestern cooking. Oily, yellowish kernels with a slight taste of resin, they can be eaten raw or toasted, ground or whole. Pine nuts are indispensible to pesto.

POLENTA: a porridge of boiled cornmeal used in Italian cooking or eaten as a side dish.

RICE SYRUP: a sweetener with a delicate taste, rice syrup is a complex carbohydrate produced by malting cooked brown rice. It is less sweet than honey, but may be used as a substitute for honey or sugar in baking and sauces.

ROUX: flour and oil cooked together to form a paste for thickening stews and soups. Rouxs are best cooked in a cast-iron skillet, over low heat for long periods. Stir often to prevent scorching, until the roux is dark brown. Salt and pepper may be added to taste. After a roux is cooked, cool it and store in a sealed jar in the fridge for future use. Whisk a few spoonfuls of cooked roux into a cup of stock or water to thicken a sauce.

SAUTÉ: to cook prepared vegetables or other food in an open skillet or pan over medium high heat in a small amount of oil, butter, or margarine, while stirring often, usually for only a few minutes at a time. Always add the oil to the skillet first and bring it to medium high heat before adding the food. Cook the food until just tender.

SCORCH: the disaster that occurs when the contents of a pot begin to burn along the bottom, leaving a brown sticky residue on the pot as well as the characteristically unpleasant smell and flavour of burned food. Avoid scorching by using heavy-bottomed pots, paying careful attention while cooking, reducing heat as needed, and stirring often. Never become so distracted that you abandon a pot over high heat. If disaster strikes, you may be able to rescue the food by immediately switching the contents to a clean pot and cooking over lower heat. If it is not too bad, a dash of sweetener or something tart, such as lemon juice or vinegar, may help mask the burned taste.

SHIITAKE MUSHROOMS: available fresh or dried, these large Japanese mushrooms have a chewy texture and a distinctive flavour. To rehydrate dried shiitakes, boil for 5 minutes, then set aside to soak for 15 to 20 minutes. Remove and discard the tough stems, and save the soaking liquid for soup.

SHOCKING: a technique of cooking pasta that allows it to cook thoroughly without becoming mushy. Bring water to a rapid boil in a large pot. Add the pasta; as soon as the water begins to boil again, add a small amount of cold water, just enough to stop the boiling. Repeat this process every time the water returns to the boil, until the pasta is cooked throughout. Although it takes a little longer, this method assures that the outer layer of pasta will not cook more quickly than the interior. Especially useful for dense or intricately shaped pastas such as rotini.

SHOYU: a Japanese soy sauce. See *Tamari* in the Guide to Seasonings, p. 221.

SHRED: to cut into very thin strips, or shreds, as in cabbage for coleslaw. Alternately, to finely grate food, such as cheese, into very small pieces.

SIMMER: to cook in a pot over low to medium heat, just below the boiling point, so that tiny bubbles form along the edges of the pan, but the food does not actively boil.

SOBA: Japanese noodles made exclusively from buckwheat flour, or from buckwheat mixed with wheat flour. When made of 100% buckwheat, soba noodles provide a delicious and useful alternative for those allergic to wheat. Popular in soups or noodle dishes, soba noodles are excellent hot or chilled.

SOYBEANS: the soybean, used extensively throughout the Orient, is a highly nutritious bean containing more protein than any other bean, in a proportion of essential amino acids close to that of animals. Indeed, this excellent and ubiquitous source of protein is known as the "boneless meat" or the "vegetable cow" of the Orient. Its bland flavour allows the soybean to slip into many recipes and beverages unnoticed, supplying a nutritional boost while taking on the flavours of the sauce, spice or marinade. In the Orient, soybeans have traditionally been ground into flour or crushed into a dairy substitute called soymilk, or aged or fermented to create *tofu, tempeh, tamari, miso,* and other soyfoods – see these individual entries for more information. Soybeans require a longer cooking time than most beans; allow them to simmer for 4 to 5 hours after soaking to render more digestible. See Dried Beans, p. 46.

In the case of the fermented soyfoods such as tempeh and miso, a mold culture is added to the soybeans, developing micro-organisms that alter the composition of the food, giving it a stronger and more pronounced flavour. Fermented foods such as tempeh or wine, cheese, sauerkraut, sourdough bread, beer, and pickles in the West, improve the intestinal flora, aiding in the digestion of dense protein and carbohydrate foods. These foods are more nutritious and digestible in their fermented state than in their unprocessed original state, and enhance the digestibility of foods consumed at the same time. In the case of high-protein soybeans, which are more difficult to digest in their natural form, the processing promotes the assimilation of their considerable nutrients.

Roasted soybeans, sometimes called soy nuts, have been commercially roasted to make a crunchy snack food.

SOYMILK: soymilk is a non-dairy beverage. This milky liquid is of special value for those who wish to avoid dairy products, either because of allergies or cholesterol. Processed from boiled soybeans, and sometimes flavoured with sweeteners or additives like vanilla or cocoa, soymilk contains no lactose, the element in milk which frequently triggers allergic reactions. Soymilk does not taste exactly like milk, but it can be substituted for milk in baking, and even in cream-based soups. Many people use it in coffee or drink it as a beverage. Several brands are available which can be stored unopened in the pantry, needing refrigeration only after opening. Use plain soymilk as the base for creamy soups, in sauces or dressings, and use the flavoured kinds for baking or drinking.

STEAM: a method of preparing food by suspending it over, boiling water: the food is cooked by the heat of the steam rising through it. Use a wide-mouthed pot with a lid, and an Oriental bamboo steamer or a metal steamer or colander. The pot should contain one half-inch to one inch of water, which should be checked during the cooking – more water may be needed to keep the pot from boiling dry. Leftover cooking water may be used in soups or sauces. Vegetables are better steamed than boiled, as fewer nutrients are lost during steaming.

STIRFRY: an Oriental method of cooking food very quickly with a small amount of hot oil in a wok or skillet, stirring almost constantly. The oil must be hot when you add the food. Items which require a longer cooking time are added first, followed by items which require less cooking. The whole procedure will take no more than 4 to 5 minutes over high heat. This leaves the vegetables flavourful and crisp. (See p. 130.)

STOCK: a broth made of water cooked with vegetables and/or peels and ends of vegetables. Used to give more flavour to soups and sauces. See p. 195 to learn how to make stock.

SUCANAT: a substitute for brown sugar, Sucanat is the brand name of a natural sweetener, the granulated form of dried cane juice. Sucanat is less refined than white granulated sugar. Substitute for equivalent amounts of white or brown sugar.

SWEETENERS: a variety of sweeteners are available at natural foods stores; *honey, maple syrup, rice syrup, Sucanat*, etc. See these entries for more information. A "sweet tooth" is a hard habit to break: experiment with alternative sweeteners that are less refined than white sugar.

TAHINI: sesame butter, a spreadable paste made from sesame seeds, is similar to but thinner in consistency than peanut butter. Rich in both calcium and flavour, tahini may be used alone as a sandwich spread, to thicken sauces and gravies, or mixed with beans to make spreads and dips such as hummus. Store in refrigerator for best results.

TEMPEH: a chewy, high-protein ingredient made from soy beans. See the section on tempeh on p. 37.

TOASTED SESAME OIL: processed from toasted sesame seeds, this oil is darker in colour than plain sesame oil, with a distinctive aroma. Use it sparingly as a flavouring agent rather than a cooking oil. Brings a potent and wonderful flavour to dressings and stirfries.

TOFU: a low-fat protein that is bland and white, almost like a cheese made from soymilk. Use in stirfries, casseroles, sandwiches, etc. See p. 25 to 29 for more information on tofu.

UDON NOODLES: thin, flat Japanese noodles made from whole wheat flour. The texture of udon noodles is particularly appropriate for chilled noodle dishes in the summer.

ZEST: the grated rind of citrus fruit (oranges, lemons, and limes, usually), used to add flavour and colour. Choose unblemished fruit that has not been sprayed with chemicals, rinse thoroughly, and grate only the uppermost layer of coloured rind, using the fine grate on a handheld grater or a special tool called a zester which peels off small strips of rind. Try not to pick up the white membrane under the coloured rind, and try not to grate the skin off your knuckles: neither adds flavour.

BIBLIOGRAPHY

By no means an exhaustive list, these are books I have found particularly helpful. Those marked with an asterisk are, to some extent, the bibles of vegetarian cooking, the classic resources that have shaped vegetarian cuisine in North America. I hope you will find this a helpful guide as you further explore the road to vegetarian cooking.

GENERAL VEGETARIAN — INFORMATION:

The following provide a wealth of helpful information about cooking and eating vegetarian meals, the staple ingredients of a vegetarian kitchen, and about the issues supporting the choice of a vegetarian diet: personal health, nutrition, animal rights, and global food distribution. Some of these books also contain recipes.

Atlas, Nava. *The Wholefood Catalog*. New York: Fawcett Columbine, 1988

*Lappé, Frances Moore. *Diet For A Small Planet* (10th Anniversary Edition). New York: Ballantine Books, 1971

Kilham, Christopher S. *The Bread & Circus Whole Food Bible*. Reading, MA: Addison-Wesley Publishing, 1991

Robbins, John. *Diet for a New America*. Walpole, NH: Stillpoint Publishing, 1987

*Robertson, Laurel et al. *The New Laurel's Kitchen*. Berkeley, CA: Ten Speed Press, 1986

Yntema, Sharon. *Vegetarian Children*. Ithaca, NY: McBooks Press, 1987

GENERAL VEGETARIAN — RECIPES:

These books, a small sampler of what's available, will provide you with a lifetime's worth of delicious recipes for cooking meatless meals. There is an ever-growing body of vegetarian cookbooks as more people come to cook and eat healthier food. Be sure to check your local natural foods store, bookstores and public library for these and other publications.

Blacker, Maryanne, ed. *Australian Women's Weekly Home Library: Vegetarian Cooking*. Sydney: Australian Consolidated Press, 1990

Brown, Edward Espe. *Tassajara Bread Book*. Boston: Shambhala Publications, 1970

Brown, Edward Espe. *Tassajara Cooking*. Berkeley, CA: Shambhala Publications, 1973

Katzen, Mollie. *The Enchanted Broccoli Forest*. Berkeley, CA: Ten Speed Press, 1982

*Katzen, Mollie. *Moosewood Cookbook*. Berkeley, CA: Ten Speed Press, 1977

Katzen, Mollie. *Still Life with Menu*. Berkeley, CA: Ten Speed Press, 1988

Lukin, Anne. *The Big Carrot Vegetarian Cookbook*. Toronto: Second Story Press, 1989

Moosewood Collective. *New Recipes from Moosewood Restaurant*. Berkeley, CA: Ten Speed Press, 1987

Shulman, Martha Rose. *Gourmet Vegetarian Feasts*. Rochester, VT: Healing Arts Press, 1990

*Thomas, Anna. *The Vegetarian Epicure*. New York: Vintage Books, 1972

INTERNATIONAL CUISINES:

Most cultures have some vegetarian dishes as part of their cuisine; many cultures around the world have lived as vegetarians for centuries. The following selection of cookbooks will introduce you to the basics of several ethnic or national cuisines. While some of these cookbooks contain meat recipes, they also abound with recipes for beans, grains, and vegetables. And they are helpful in uncovering the predominant flavours, spicings, and kitchen secrets of other cuisines; it will be up to you to adapt that information for your own vegetarian cooking.

Atlas, Nava. *American Harvest (Regional Recipes for the Vegetarian Kitchen)*. New York: Fawcett Columbine, 1987

Chaitow, Alkmini. *Greek Vegetarian Cooking*. Rochester, VT: Healing Arts Press, 1984

East West Journal, ed. *Whole World Cookbook (International Macrobiotic Cuisine)*. Wayne, NJ: Avery Publishing Group, Inc., 1984

Hazan, Marcella. *The Classic Italian Cookbook*. New York: Ballantine Books, 1973

Jaffreys, Madhur. *Far Eastern Cookery*. New York: Harper & Row, 1989

*Jaffreys, Madhur. *World-of-the-East Vegetarian Cooking*. New York: Alfred A. Knopf, 1981

Karoff, Barbara. *South American Cooking (Foods & Feasts from the New World)*. Berkeley, CA: Aris Books, 1989

Levy, Faye. *Fresh From France, Vegetable Creations*. New York: E.P. Dutton, 1987

Moosewood Collective. *Sundays at Moosewood Restaurant*. New York: Simon and Schuster Fireside, 1990

Ortiz, Elizabeth Lambert. *The Complete Book of Mexican Cooking*. New York: Ballantine Books, 1967

Wells, Troth. *The New Internationalist Food Book*. Toronto: Second Story Press, 1990

SPECIALTY BOOKS *(macrobiotics, cooking with tofu, allergies, diets, etc.)*:

Bates, Dorothy. *The Tempeh Cookbook*. Summertown, TN: The Book Publishing Co., 1989

Colbin, Annemarie. *The Natural Gourmet*. New York: Ballantine Books, 1989

Greenberg, Ron and Nori, Angela. *Freedom From Allergy Cookbook*. Vancouver: Blue Poppy Press, 1988

Hartung, Shirley. *Cookies Naturally*. Kitchener, ON: Cookies Naturally, 1989

Klape, Michael, M.D. *Vegan Nutrition: Pure and Simple*. Umatilla, FL: Gentle World, Inc., 1987

Kushi, Michio. *The Macrobiotic Way*. Wayne, NJ: Avery Publishing, 1985

Shurtleff, William and Aoyagi, Akiko. *The Book of Tofu*. New York: Ballantine Books, 1975

MISCELLANEOUS:

Button, John. *How To Be Green*. London: Random Century Ltd., 1989

Earth Works Group. *The Recyclers Handbook*. Berkeley, CA: Earth Works Press, 1990

Lindsay, Anne. *The Lighthearted Cookbook*. Toronto: Key Porter Books, 1988

Lindsay, Anne. *Smart Cooking*. Toronto: Macmillan of Canada, 1986

Miles, Karen. *Herb & Spice Handbook*. Norway, IA: Frontier Cooperative Herbs, 1987

Pollution Probe Foundation. *The Canadian Green Consumer Guide*. Toronto: McClelland & Stewart, 1989

Seiden, Dr. Howard S. *Getting to the Heart of Cholesterol*. Toronto: Grosvenor House Press, Inc., 1989

INDEX